MW01468953

the FMLA handbook

DOCUMENTARY APPENDIX

WORK RIGHTS PRESS

Cambridge, Massachusetts

Also available from Work Rights Press:

The FMLA Handbook: A Practical Guide to the Family and Medical Leave Act for Union Members and Stewards by Robert M. Schwartz ($9.95 plus $2.00 postage).

The Legal Rights of Union Stewards by Robert M. Schwartz ($9.95 plus $2.00 postage).

How to Win Past Practice Grievances by Robert M. Schwartz ($9.95 plus $2.00 postage).

Work Rights Press
P.O. 391887
Cambridge, MA 02139-0008

Telephone: 1-800-576-4552

APPENDICES

APPENDIX A

THE FAMILY AND MEDICAL LEAVE ACT OF 1993, TITLES I, III AND IV

29 U.S.C. §§ 2601, 2611–2619, 2631–2636 and 2651–2654

29 U.S.C § 2601. Findings and purposes

(a) Findings. Congress finds that —

(1) the number of single-parent households and two-parent households in which the single parent or both parents work is increasing significantly;

(2) it is important for the development of children and the family unit that fathers and mothers be able to participate in early childrearing and the care of family members who have serious health conditions;

(3) the lack of employment policies to accommodate working parents can force individuals to choose between job security and parenting;

(4) there is inadequate job security for employees who have serious health conditions that prevent them from working for temporary periods;

(5) due to the nature of the roles of men and women in our society, the primary responsibility for family caretaking often falls on women, and such responsibility affects the working lives of women more than it affects the working lives of men; and

(6) employment standards that apply to one gender only have serious potential for encouraging employers to discriminate against employees and applicants for employment who are of that gender.

(b) Purposes. It is the purpose of this Act —

(1) to balance the demands of the workplace with the needs of families, to promote the stability and economic security of families, and to promote national interests in preserving family integrity;

(2) to entitle employees to take reasonable leave for medical reasons, for the birth or adoption of a child, and for the care of a child, spouse, or parent who has a serious health condition;

(3) to accomplish the purposes described in paragraphs (1) and (2) in a manner that accommodates the legitimate interests of employers;

(4) to accomplish the purposes described in paragraphs (1) and (2) in a

manner that, consistent with the Equal Protection Clause of the Fourteenth Amendment minimizes the potential for employment discrimination on the basis of sex by ensuring generally that leave is available for eligible medical reasons (including maternity-related disability) and for compelling family reasons, on a gender-neutral basis; and

(5) to promote the goal of equal employment opportunity for women and men, pursuant to such clause.

TITLE I: GENERAL REQUIREMENTS FOR LEAVE

29 U.S.C. § 2611. Definitions

As used in this title:

(1) *Commerce.* The terms "commerce" and "industry or activity affecting commerce" mean any activity, business, or industry in commerce or in which a labor dispute would hinder or obstruct commerce or the free flow of commerce, and include "commerce" and any "industry affecting commerce", as defined in paragraphs (1) and (3) of section 501 of the Labor Management Relations Act, 1947 (29 U.S.C. 142 (1) and (3)).

(2) *Eligible employee.*

(A) In general. The term "eligible employee" means an employee who has been employed —

(i) for at least 12 months by the employer with respect to whom leave is requested under section 2612 of this title; and

(ii) for at least 1,250 hours of service with such employer during the previous 12-month period.

(B) Exclusions. The term "eligible employee" does not include —

(i) any Federal officer or employee covered under subchapter V of chapter 63 of title 5, United States Code (as added by title II of this Act); or

(ii) any employee of an employer who is employed at a worksite at which such employer employs less than 50 employees if the total number of employees employed by that employer within 75 miles of that worksite is less than 50.

(C) Determination. For purposes of determining whether an employee meets the hours of service requirement specified in subparagraph (A)(ii), the legal standards established under section 7 of the Fair Labor Standards Act of 1938 (29 U.S.C. 207) shall apply.

(3) *Employ; employee; State.* The terms "employ", "employee", and "State" have the same meanings given such terms in subsections (c), (e), and (g) of section 3 of the Fair Labor Standards Act of 1938 (29 U.S.C. 203 (c), (e), and (g)).

(4) *Employer.*

(A) In general. The term "employer" —

(i) means any person engaged in commerce or in any industry or activity affecting commerce who employs 50 or more employees for each working day during each of 20 or more calendar workweeks in the current or preceding calendar year;

(ii) includes —

(I) any person who acts, directly or indirectly, in the interest of an employer to any of the employees of such employer; and

(II) any successor in interest of an employer; and

(iii) includes any "public agency", as defined in section 3(x) of the Fair Labor Standards Act of 1938 (29 U.S.C. 203(x)).

(B) Public agency. For purposes of subparagraph (A)(iii), a public agency shall be considered to be a person engaged in commerce or in an industry or activity affecting commerce.

(5) *Employment benefits.* The term "employment benefits" means all benefits provided or made available to employees by an employer, including group life insurance, health insurance, disability insurance, sick leave, annual leave, educational benefits, and pensions, regardless of whether such benefits are provided by a practice or written policy of an employer or through an "employee benefit plan", as defined in section 3(3) of the Employee Retirement Income Security Act of 1974 (29 U.S.C. 1002(3)).

(6) *Health care provider.* The term "health care provider" means —

(A) a doctor of medicine or osteopathy who is authorized to practice medicine or surgery (as appropriate) by the State in which the doctor practices; or

(B) any other person determined by the Secretary to be capable of providing health care services.

(7) *Parent.* The term "parent" means the biological parent of an employee or an individual who stood *in loco parentis* to an employee when the employee was a son or daughter.

(8) *Person.* The term "person" has the same meaning given such term in section 3(a) of the Fair Labor Standards Act of 1938 (29 U.S.C. 203(a)).

(9) *Reduced leave schedule.* The term "reduced leave schedule" means a leave schedule that reduces the usual number of hours per workweek, or hours per workday, of an employee.

(10) *Secretary.* The term "Secretary" means the Secretary of Labor.

(11) *Serious health condition.* The term "serious health condition" means an illness, injury, impairment, or physical or mental condition that involves —

(A) inpatient care in a hospital, hospice, or residential medical care facility; or

(B) continuing treatment by a health care provider.

(12) *Son or daughter.* The term "son or daughter" means a biological, adopted, or foster child, a stepchild, a legal ward, or a child of a person standing *in loco parentis*, who is —

(A) under 18 years of age; or

(B) 18 years of age or older and incapable of self-care because of a mental or physical disability.

(13) *Spouse.* The term "spouse" means a husband or wife, as the case may be.

29 U.S.C. § 2612. Leave requirement

(a) In general.

(1) Entitlement to leave. Subject to section 2613 of this title, an eligible employee shall be entitled to a total of 12 workweeks of leave during any 12-month period for one or more of the following:

(A) Because of the birth of a son or daughter of the employee and in order to care for such son or daughter.

(B) Because of the placement of a son or daughter with the employee for adoption or foster care.

(C) In order to care for the spouse, or a son, daughter, or parent, of the employee, if such spouse, son, daughter, or parent has a serious health condition.

(D) Because of a serious health condition that makes the employee unable to perform the functions of the position of such employee.

(2) Expiration of entitlement. The entitlement to leave under subparagraphs (A) and (B) of paragraph (1) for a birth or placement of a son or daughter shall expire at the end of the 12-month period beginning on the date of such birth or placement.

(b) Leave taken intermittently or on a reduced leave schedule.

(1) In general. Leave under subparagraph (A) or (B) of subsection (a)(1) shall not be taken by an employee intermittently or on a reduced leave schedule unless the employee and the employer of the employee agree otherwise. Subject to paragraph (2), subsection (e)(2) and section 2613(b)(5) of this title, leave under subparagraph (C) or (D) of subsection (a)(1) may be taken intermittently or on a reduced leave schedule when medically necessary. The taking of leave intermittently or on a reduced leave schedule pursuant to this paragraph shall not result in a reduction in the total amount of leave to which the employee is entitled under subsection (a) beyond the amount of leave actually taken.

(2) Alternative position. If an employee requests intermittent leave, or leave on a reduced leave schedule, under subparagraph (C) or (D) of subsection (a)(1), that is foreseeable based on planned medical treatment, the employer may require such employee to transfer temporarily to an available alternative position offered by the employer for which the employee is qualified and that —

(A) has equivalent pay and benefits; and

(B) better accommodates recurring periods of leave than the regular employment position of the employee.

(c) Unpaid leave permitted. Except as provided in subsection (d), leave granted under subsection (a) may consist of unpaid leave. Where an employee is otherwise exempt under regulations issued by the Secretary pursuant to section 13(a)(1) of the Fair Labor Standards Act of 1938 (29 U.S.C. 213(a)(1)), the compliance of an employer with this title by providing unpaid leave shall not affect the exempt status of the employee under such section.

(d) Relationship to paid leave.

(1) Unpaid leave. If an employer provides paid leave for fewer than 12 workweeks, the additional weeks of leave necessary to attain the 12 workweeks of leave required under this title may be provided without compensation.

(2) Substitution of paid leave.

(A) In general. An eligible employee may elect, or an employer may require the employee, to substitute any of the accrued paid vacation leave, personal leave, or family leave of the employee for leave provided under subparagraph (A), (B), or (C) of subsection (a)(1) for any part of the 12-week period of such leave under such subsection.

(B) Serious health condition. An eligible employee may elect, or an employer may require the employee, to substitute any of the accrued paid vacation leave, personal leave, or medical or sick leave of the employee for leave provided under subparagraph (C) or (D) of subsection (a)(1) for any part of the 12-week period of such leave under such subsection, except that nothing in this title shall require an employer to provide paid sick leave or paid medical leave in any situation in which such employer would not normally provide any such paid leave.

(e) Foreseeable leave.

(1) Requirement of notice. In any case in which the necessity for leave under subparagraph (A) or (B) of subsection (a)(1) is foreseeable based on an expected birth or placement, the employee shall provide the employer with not less than 30 days' notice, before the date the leave is to begin, of the employee's intention to take leave under such subparagraph, except that if the date of the birth or placement requires leave to begin in less than 30 days, the employee shall provide such notice as is practicable.

(2) Duties of employee. In any case in which the necessity for leave under subparagraph (C) or (D) of subsection (a)(1) is foreseeable based on planned medical treatment, the employee —

(A) shall make a reasonable effort to schedule the treatment so as not to disrupt unduly the operations of the employer, subject to the approval of the health care provider of the employee or the health care provider of the son, daughter, spouse, or parent of the employee, as appropriate; and

(B) shall provide the employer with not less than 30 days' notice, before the date the leave is to begin, of the employee's intention to take leave under such subparagraph, except that if the date of the treatment requires leave to begin in less than 30 days, the employee shall provide such notice as is practicable.

(f) Spouses employed by the same employer. In any case in which a husband and wife entitled to leave under subsection (a) are employed by the same employer, the aggregate number of workweeks of leave to which both may be entitled may be limited to 12 workweeks during any 12-month period, if such leave is taken —

(1) under subparagraph (A) or (B) of subsection (a)(1); or

(2) to care for a sick parent under subparagraph (C) of such subsection.

29 U.S.C. § 2613. Certification

(a) In general. An employer may require that a request for leave under subparagraph (C) or (D) of section 2612(a)(1) of this title be supported by a certification issued by the health care provider of the eligible employee or of the son, daughter, spouse, or parent of the employee, as appropriate. The employee shall provide, in a timely manner, a copy of such certification to the employer.

(b) Sufficient certification. Certification provided under subsection (a) shall be sufficient if it states —

(1) the date on which the serious health condition commenced;

(2) the probable duration of the condition;

(3) the appropriate medical facts within the knowledge of the health care provider regarding the condition;

(4)(A) for purposes of leave under section 2612(a)(1)(C) of this title, a statement that the eligible employee is needed to care for the son, daughter, spouse, or parent and an estimate of the amount of time that such employee is needed to care for the son, daughter, spouse, or parent; and

(B) for purposes of leave under section 2612(a)(1)(D)] of this title, a statement that the employee is unable to perform the functions of the position of the employee;

(5) in the case of certification for intermittent leave, or leave on a reduced leave schedule, for planned medical treatment, the dates on which such treatment is expected to be given and the duration of such treatment;

(6) in the case of certification for intermittent leave, or leave on a reduced leave schedule, under section 2612(a)(1)(D) of this title, a statement of the medical necessity for the intermittent leave or leave on a reduced leave schedule, and the expected duration of the intermittent leave or reduced leave schedule; and

(7) in the case of certification for intermittent leave, or leave on a reduced leave schedule, under section 2612(a)(1)(C) of this title, a statement that the employee's intermittent leave or leave on a reduced leave schedule is necessary for the care of the son, daughter, parent, or spouse who has a serious health condition, or will assist in their recovery, and the expected duration and schedule of the intermittent leave or reduced leave schedule.

(c) Second opinion.

(1) In general. In any case in which the employer has reason to doubt the validity of the certification provided under subsection (a) for leave under sub-paragraph (C) or (D) of section 2612(a)(1) of this title, the employer may require, at the expense of the employer, that the eligible employee obtain the opinion of a second health care provider designated or approved by the employer concerning any information certified under subsection (b) for such leave.

(2) Limitation. A health care provider designated or approved under paragraph (1) shall not be employed on a regular basis by the employer.

(d) Resolution of conflicting opinions.

(1) In general. In any case in which the second opinion described in subsection (c) differs from the opinion in the original certification provided under subsection (a), the employer may require, at the expense of the employer, that the employee obtain the opinion of a third health care provider designated or approved jointly by the employer and the employee concerning the information certified under subsection (b).

(2) Finality. The opinion of the third health care provider concerning the information certified under subsection (b) shall be considered to be final and shall be binding on the employer and the employee.

(e) Subsequent recertification. The employer may require that the eligible employee obtain subsequent recertifications on a reasonable basis.

29 U.S.C. § 2614. Employment and benefits protection

(a) Restoration to position.

(1) In general. Except as provided in subsection (b), any eligible employee who takes leave under section 2612 of this title for the intended purpose of the leave shall be entitled, on return from such leave —

(A) to be restored by the employer to the position of employment held by the employee when the leave commenced; or

(B) to be restored to an equivalent position with equivalent employment benefits, pay, and other terms and conditions of employment.

(2) Loss of benefits. The taking of leave under section 2612 of this title shall not result in the loss of any employment benefit accrued prior to the date on which the leave commenced.

(3) Limitations. Nothing in this section shall be construed to entitle any restored employee to —

(A) the accrual of any seniority or employment benefits during any period of leave; or

(B) any right, benefit, or position of employment other than any right, benefit, or position to which the employee would have been entitled had the employee not taken the leave.

(4) Certification. As a condition of restoration under paragraph (1) for an employee who has taken leave under section 2612(a)(1)(D) of this title, the employer may have a uniformly applied practice or policy that requires each such employee to receive certification from the health care provider of the employee that the employee is able to resume work, except that nothing in this paragraph shall supersede a valid State or local law or a collective bargaining agreement that governs the return to work of such employees.

(5) Construction. Nothing in this subsection shall be construed to prohibit an employer from requiring an employee on leave under section 2612 of this title to report periodically to the employer on the status and intention of the employee to return to work.

(b) Exemption concerning certain highly compensated employees.

(1) Denial of restoration. An employer may deny restoration under subsection (a) to any eligible employee described in paragraph (2) if —

(A) such denial is necessary to prevent substantial and grievous economic injury to the operations of the employer;

(B) the employer notifies the employee of the intent of the employer to deny restoration on such basis at the time the employer determines that such injury would occur; and

(C) in any case in which the leave has commenced, the employee elects not to return to employment after receiving such notice.

(2) Affected employees. An eligible employee described in paragraph (1) is a salaried eligible employee who is among the highest paid 10 percent of the employees employed by the employer within 75 miles of the facility at which the employee is employed.

(c) Maintenance of health benefits.

(1) Coverage. Except as provided in paragraph (2), during any period that an eligible employee takes leave under section 2612 of this title, the employer shall maintain coverage under any "group health plan" (as defined in sec-

tion 5000(b)(1) of the Internal Revenue Code of 1986) for the duration of such leave at the level and under the conditions coverage would have been provided if the employee had continued in employment continuously for the duration of such leave.

(2) Failure to return from leave. The employer may recover the premium that the employer paid for maintaining coverage for the employee under such group health plan during any period of unpaid leave under section 2612 of this title if —

(A) the employee fails to return from leave under section 2612 of this title after the period of leave to which the employee is entitled has expired; and

(B) the employee fails to return to work for a reason other than —

(i) the continuation, recurrence, or onset of a serious health condition that entitles the employee to leave under subparagraph (C) or (D) of section 2612(a)(1) of this title; or

(ii) other circumstances beyond the control of the employee.

(3) Certification.

(A) Issuance. An employer may require that a claim that an employee is unable to return to work because of the continuation, recurrence, or onset of the serious health condition described in paragraph (2)(B)(i) be supported by —

(i) a certification issued by the health care provider of the son, daughter, spouse, or parent of the employee, as appropriate, in the case of an employee unable to return to work because of a condition specified in section 2612(a)(1)(C) of this title; or

(ii) a certification issued by the health care provider of the eligible employee, in the case of an employee unable to return to work because of a condition specified in section 2612(a)(1)(D) of this title.

(B) Copy. The employee shall provide, in a timely manner, a copy of such certification to the employer.

(C) Sufficiency of certification.

(i) Leave due to serious health condition of employee. The certification described in subparagraph (A)(ii) shall be sufficient if the certification states that a serious health condition prevented the employee from being able to perform the functions of the position of the employee on the date that the leave of the employee expired.

(ii) Leave due to serious health condition of family member. The certification described in subparagraph (A)(i) shall be sufficient if the certification states that the employee is needed to care for the son, daughter, spouse, or parent who has a serious health condition on the date that the leave of the employee expired.

29 U.S.C. § 2615. Prohibited acts

(a) Interference with rights.

(1) Exercise of rights. It shall be unlawful for any employer to interfere with, restrain, or deny the exercise of or the attempt to exercise, any right provided under this title.

(2) Discrimination. It shall be unlawful for any employer to discharge or in any other manner discriminate against any individual for opposing any practice made unlawful by this title.

(b) Interference with proceedings or inquiries. It shall be unlawful for any person to discharge or in any other manner discriminate against any individual because such individual —

(1) has filed any charge, or has instituted or caused to be instituted any proceeding, under or related to this title;

(2) has given, or is about to give, any information in connection with any inquiry or proceeding relating to any right provided under this title; or

(3) has testified, or is about to testify, in any inquiry or proceeding relating to any right provided under this title.

29 U.S.C. § 2616. Investigative authority

(a) In general. To ensure compliance with the provisions of this title, or any regulation or order issued under this title, the Secretary shall have, subject to subsection (c), the investigative authority provided under section 11(a) of the Fair Labor Standards Act of 1938 (29 U.S.C. 211(a)).

(b) Obligation to keep and preserve records. Any employer shall make, keep, and preserve records pertaining to compliance with this title in accordance with section 11(c) of the Fair Labor Standards Act of 1938 (29 U.S.C. 211(c)) and in accordance with regulations issued by the Secretary.

(c) Required submissions generally limited to an annual basis. The Secretary shall not under the authority of this section require any employer or any plan, fund, or program to submit to the Secretary any books or records more than once during any 12-month period, unless the Secretary has reasonable cause to believe there may exist a violation of this title or any regulation or order issued pursuant to this title, or is investigating a charge pursuant to section 2617(b) of this title.

(d) Subpoena powers. For the purposes of any investigation provided for in this section, the Secretary shall have the subpoena authority provided for under section 9 of the Fair Labor Standards Act of 1938 (29 U.S.C. 209).

U.S.C. § 2617. Enforcement

(a) Civil action by employees.

(1) Liability. Any employer who violates section 2615 of this title shall be liable to any eligible employee affected —

(A) for damages equal to —

(i) the amount of —

(I) any wages, salary, employment benefits, or other compensation denied or lost to such employee by reason of the violation; or

(II) in a case in which wages, salary, employment benefits, or other compensation have not been denied or lost to the employee, any actual monetary losses sustained by the employee as a direct result of the violation, such as the cost of providing care, up to a sum equal to 12 weeks of wages or salary for the employee;

(ii) the interest on the amount described in clause (i) calculated at the prevailing rate; and

(iii) an additional amount as liquidated damages equal to the sum of the amount described in clause (i) and the interest described in clause (ii), except that if an employer who has violated section 2615 of this title proves to the satisfaction of the court that the act or omission which violated section 2615 of this title was in good faith and that the employer had reasonable grounds for believing that the act or omission was not a violation of section 2615 of this title, such court may, in the discretion of the court, reduce the amount of the liability to the amount and interest determined under clauses (i) and (ii), respectively; and

(B) for such equitable relief as may be appropriate, including employment, reinstatement, and promotion.

(2) Right of action. An action to recover the damages or equitable relief prescribed in paragraph (1) may be maintained against any employer (including a public agency) in any Federal or State court of competent jurisdiction by any one or more employees for and in behalf of —

(A) the employees; or

(B) the employees and other employees similarly situated.

(3) Fees and costs. The court in such an action shall, in addition to any judgment awarded to the plaintiff, allow a reasonable attorney's fee, reasonable expert witness fees, and other costs of the action to be paid by the defendant.

(4) Limitations. The right provided by paragraph (2) to bring an action by or on behalf of any employee shall terminate —

(A) on the filing of a complaint by the Secretary in an action under subsection (d) in which restraint is sought of any further delay in the payment of the amount described in paragraph (1)(A) to such employee by an employer responsible under paragraph (1) for the payment; or

(B) on the filing of a complaint by the Secretary in an action under subsection (b) in which a recovery is sought of the damages described in paragraph (1)(A) owing to an eligible employee by an employer liable under paragraph (1), unless the action described in subparagraph (A) or (B) is dismissed without prejudice on motion of the Secretary.

(b) Action by the Secretary.

(1) Administrative action. The Secretary shall receive, investigate, and attempt to resolve complaints of violations of section 105 in the same manner that the Secretary receives, investigates, and attempts to resolve complaints of violations of sections 6 and 7 of the Fair Labor Standards Act of 1938 (29 U.S.C. 206 and 207).

(2) Civil action. The Secretary may bring an action in any court of competent jurisdiction to recover the damages described in subsection (a)(1)(A).

(3) Sums recovered. Any sums recovered by the Secretary pursuant to paragraph (2) shall be held in a special deposit account and shall be paid, on order of the Secretary, directly to each employee affected. Any such sums not paid to an employee because of inability to do so within a period of 3 years shall be deposited into the Treasury of the United States as miscellaneous receipts.

(c) Limitation.

(1) In general. Except as provided in paragraph (2), an action may be brought under this section not later than 2 years after the date of the last event constituting the alleged violation for which the action is brought.

(2) Willful violation. In the case of such action brought for a willful violation of section 2615 of this title, such action may be brought within 3 years of the date of the last event constituting the alleged violation for which such action is brought.

(3) Commencement. In determining when an action is commenced by the Secretary under this section for the purposes of this subsection, it shall be considered to be commenced on the date when the complaint is filed.

(d) Action for injunction by Secretary. The district courts of the United States shall have jurisdiction, for cause shown, in an action brought by the Secretary —

(1) to restrain violations of section 2615 of the title, including the restraint of any withholding of payment of wages, salary, employment benefits, or other compensation, plus interest, found by the court to be due to eligible employees; or

(2) to award such other equitable relief as may be appropriate, including employment, reinstatement, and promotion.

(e) Solicitor of Labor. The Solicitor of Labor may appear for and represent the Secretary on any litigation brought under this section.

29 U.S.C. § 2618. Special rules concerning employees of local educational agencies

(a) Application.

(1) In general. Except as otherwise provided in this section, the rights (including the rights under section 2614 of this title which shall extend

throughout the period of leave of any employee under this section), remedies, and procedures under this title shall apply to —

(A) any "local educational agency" (as defined in section 14101 of the Elementary and Secondary Education Act of 1965 (20 U.S.C. 2891(12)) and an eligible employee of the agency; and

(B) any private elementary or secondary school and an eligible employee of the school.

(2) Definitions. For purposes of the application described in paragraph (1):

(A) Eligible employee. The term "eligible employee" means an eligible employee of an agency or school described in paragraph (1).

(B) Employer. The term "employer" means an agency or school described in paragraph (1).

(b) Leave does not violate certain other Federal laws. A local educational agency and a private elementary or secondary school shall not be in violation of the Individuals with Disabilities Education Act (20 U.S.C. 1400 *et seq.*), section 504 of the Rehabilitation Act of 1973 (29 U.S.C. 794), or title VI of the Civil Rights Act of 1964 (42 U.S.C. 2000d *et seq.*), solely as a result of an eligible employee of such agency or school exercising the rights of such employee under this title.

(c) Intermittent leave or leave on a reduced schedule for instructional employees.

(1) In general. Subject to paragraph (2), in any case in which an eligible employee employed principally in an instructional capacity by any such educational agency or school requests leave under subparagraph (C) or (D) of section 2612(a)(1) of this title that is foreseeable based on planned medical treatment and the employee would be on leave for greater than 20 percent of the total number of working days in the period during which the leave would extend, the agency or school may require that such employee elect either —

(A) to take leave for periods of a particular duration, not to exceed the duration of the planned medical treatment; or

(B) to transfer temporarily to an available alternative position offered by the employer for which the employee is qualified, and that —

(i) has equivalent pay and benefits; and

(ii) better accommodates recurring periods of leave than the regular employment position of the employee.

(2) Application. The elections described in subparagraphs (A) and (B) of paragraph (1) shall apply only with respect to an eligible employee who complies with section 2612(e)(2) of this title.

(d) Rules applicable to periods near the conclusion of an academic term. The following rules shall apply with respect to periods of leave near the conclusion of an academic term in the case of any eligible employee employed principally in an instructional capacity by any such educational agency or school:

(1) Leave more than 5 weeks prior to end of term. If the eligible employee begins leave under section 2612 of this title more than 5 weeks prior to the end of the academic term, the agency or school may require the employee to continue taking leave until the end of such term, if —

(A) the leave is of at least 3 weeks duration; and

(B) the return to employment would occur during the 3-week period before the end of such term.

(2) Leave less than 5 weeks prior to end of term. If the eligible employee begins leave under subparagraph (A), (B), or (C) of section 2612(a)(1) of this title during the period that commences 5 weeks prior to the end of the academic term, the agency or school may require the employee to continue taking leave until the end of such term, if —

(A) the leave is of greater than 2 weeks duration; and

(B) the return to employment would occur during the 2-week period before the end of such term.

(3) Leave less than 3 weeks prior to end of term. If the eligible employee begins leave under subparagraph (A), (B), or (C) of section 2612(a)(1) of this title during the period that commences 3 weeks prior to the end of the academic term and the duration of the leave is greater than 5 working days, the agency or school may require the employee to continue to take leave until the end of such term.

(e) Restoration to equivalent employment position. For purposes of determinations under section 2614(a)(1)(B) of this title (relating to the restoration of an eligible employee to an equivalent position), in the case of a local educational agency or a private elementary or secondary school, such determination shall be made on the basis of established school board policies and practices, private school policies and practices, and collective bargaining agreements.

(f) Reduction of the amount of liability. If a local educational agency or a private elementary or secondary school that has violated this title proves to the satisfaction of the court that the agency, school, or department had reasonable grounds for believing that the underlying act or omission was not a violation of this title such court may, in the discretion of the court, reduce the amount of the liability provided for under section 2617(a)(1)(A) of this title to the amount and interest determined under clauses (i) and (ii), respectively, of such section.

29 U.S.C. § 2619. Notice

(a) In general. Each employer shall post and keep posted, in conspicuous places on the premises of the employer where notices to employees and applicants for employment are customarily posted, a notice, to be prepared or approved by the Secretary, setting forth excerpts from, or summaries of, the pertinent provisions of this title and information pertaining to the filing of a charge.

(b) Penalty. Any employer that willfully violates this section may be assessed a civil money penalty not to exceed $100 for each separate offense.

TITLE III: COMMISSION ON LEAVE

29 U.S.C. § 2631. Establishment

There is established a commission to be known as the Commission on Leave (referred to in this title as the "Commission").

29 U.S. C. § 2632. Duties

The Commission shall —

(1) conduct a comprehensive study of —

(A) existing and proposed mandatory and voluntary policies relating to family and temporary medical leave, including policies provided by employers not covered under this Act;

(B) the potential costs, benefits, and impact on productivity, job creation and business growth of such policies on employers and employees;

(C) possible differences in costs, benefits, and impact on productivity, job creation and business growth of such policies on employers based on business type and size;

(D) the impact of family and medical leave policies on the availability of employee benefits provided by employers, including employers not covered under this Act;

(E) alternate and equivalent State enforcement of title I with respect to employees described in section 2618(a) of this title;

(F) methods used by employers to reduce administrative costs of implementing family and medical leave policies;

(G) the ability of the employers to recover, under section 2614(c)(2) of this title, the premiums described in such section; and

(H) the impact on employers and employees of policies that provide temporary wage replacement during periods of family and medical leave.

(2) not later than 2 years after the date on which the Commission first meets, prepare and submit, to the appropriate Committees of Congress, a report concerning the subjects listed in paragraph (1).

29 U.S.C. § 2633. Membership

(a) Composition.

(1) Appointments. The Commission shall be composed of 12 voting members and 4 ex officio members to be appointed not later than 60 days after the date of the enactment of this Act [Feb. 5, 1993] as follows:

(A) Senators. One Senator shall be appointed by the Majority Leader of the Senate, and one Senator shall be appointed by the Minority Leader of the Senate.

(B) Members of House of Representatives. One Member of the House of Representatives shall be appointed by the Speaker of the House of Representatives, and one Member of the House of Representatives shall be appointed by the Minority Leader of the House of Representatives.

(C) Additional members.

(i) Appointment. Two members each shall be appointed by —

(I) the Speaker of the House of Representatives;

(II) the Majority Leader of the Senate;

(III) the Minority Leader of the House of Representatives; and

(IV) the Minority Leader of the Senate.

(ii) Expertise. Such members shall be appointed by virtue of demonstrated expertise in relevant family, temporary disability, and labor management issues. Such members shall include representatives of employers, including employers from large businesses and from small businesses.

(2) Ex officio members. The Secretary of Health and Human Services, the Secretary of Labor, the Secretary of Commerce, and the Administrator of the Small Business Administration shall serve on the Commission as non-voting ex officio members.

(b) Vacancies. Any vacancy on the Commission shall be filled in the manner in which the original appointment was made. The vacancy shall not affect the power of the remaining members to execute the duties of the Commission.

(c) Chairperson and vice chairperson. The Commission shall elect a chairperson and a vice chairperson from among the members of the Commission.

(d) Quorum. Eight members of the Commission shall constitute a quorum for all purposes, except that a lesser number may constitute a quorum for the purpose of holding hearings.

29 U.S.C. § 2634. Compensation

(a) Pay. Members of the Commission shall serve without compensation.

(b) Travel expenses. Members of the Commission shall be allowed reasonable travel expenses, including a per diem allowance, in accordance with section 5703 of title 5, United States Code, when performing duties of the Commission.

29 U.S.C. § 2635. Powers

(a) Meetings. The Commission shall first meet not later than 30 days after the date on which all members are appointed, and the Commission shall meet thereafter on the call of the chairperson or a majority of the members.

(b) Hearings and sessions. The Commission may hold such hearings, sit and act at such times and places, take such testimony, and receive such evidence as the Commission considers appropriate. The Commission may administer oaths or affirmations to witnesses appearing before it.

(c) Access to information. The Commission may secure directly from any Federal agency information necessary to enable it to carry out this title, if the information may be disclosed under section 552 of title 5, United States Code. Subject to the previous sentence, on the request of the chairperson or vice chairperson of the Commission, the head of such agency shall furnish such information to the Commission.

(d) Use of facilities and services. Upon the request of the Commission, the head of any Federal agency may make available to the Commission any of the facilities and services of such agency.

(e) Personnel from other agencies. On the request of the Commission, the head of any Federal agency may detail any of the personnel of such agency to serve as an Executive Director of the Commission or assist the Commission in carrying out the duties of the Commission. Any detail shall not interrupt or otherwise affect the civil service status or privileges of the Federal employee.

(f) Voluntary service. Notwithstanding section 1342 of title 31, United States Code, the chairperson of the Commission may accept for the Commission voluntary services provided by a member of the Commission.

29 U.S.C. § 2636. Termination

The Commission shall terminate 30 days after the date of the submission of the report of the Commission to Congress.

TITLE IV: MISCELLANEOUS PROVISIONS

29 U.S.C. § 2651. Effect on other laws

(a) Federal and State antidiscrimination laws. Nothing in this Act or any amendment made by this Act shall be construed to modify or affect any Federal or State law prohibiting discrimination on the basis of race, religion, color, national origin, sex, age, or disability.

(b) State and local laws. Nothing in this Act or any amendment made by this Act shall be construed to supersede any provision of any State or local law that provides greater family or medical leave rights than the rights established under this Act or any amendment made by this Act.

29 U.S. C. § 2652. Effect on existing employment benefits

(a) More protective. Nothing in this Act or any amendment made by this Act shall be construed to diminish the obligation of an employer to comply with any collective bargaining agreement or any employment benefit program or plan that provides greater family or medical leave rights to employees than the rights established under this Act or any amendment made by this Act.

(b) Less protective. The rights established for employees under this Act or any amendment made by this Act shall not be diminished by any collective bargaining agreement or any employment benefit program or plan.

29 U.S.C. § 2653. Encouragement of more generous leave policies

Nothing in this Act or any amendment made by this Act shall be construed to discourage employers from adopting or retaining leave policies more generous than any policies that comply with the requirements under this Act or any amendment made by this Act.

29 U.S.C. § 2654. Regulations

The Secretary of Labor shall prescribe such regulations as are necessary to carry out title I and this title not later than 120 days after the date of the enactment of this Act [Feb. 5, 1993]

APPENDIX B

THE FAMILY AND MEDICAL LEAVE ACT OF 1993, TITLE II (COVERING FEDERAL EMPLOYEES)

5 U.S.C. §§ 6381–6387
SUBCHAPTER V
FAMILY AND MEDICAL LEAVE

5 U.S.C. § 6381. Definitions

For the purpose of this subchapter —

(1) the term "employee" means any individual who —

(A) is an "employee", as defined by section 6301(2), including any individual employed in a position referred to in clause (v) or (ix) of section 6301(2), but excluding any individual employed by the government of the District of Columbia and any individual employed on a temporary or intermittent basis; and

(B) has completed at least 12 months of service as an employee (within the meaning of subparagraph (A));

(2) the term "health care provider" means —

(A) a doctor of medicine or osteopathy who is authorized to practice medicine or surgery (as appropriate) by the State in which the doctor practices; and

(B) any other person determined by the Director of the Office of Personnel Management to be capable of providing health care services;

(3) the term "parent" means the biological parent of an employee or an individual who stood *in loco parentis* to an employee when the employee was a son or daughter;

(4) the term "reduced leave schedule" means a leave schedule that reduces the usual number of hours per workweek, or hours per workday, of an employee;

(5) the term "serious health condition" means an illness, injury, impairment, or physical or mental condition that involves —

(A) inpatient care in a hospital, hospice, or residential medical care facility; or

(B) continuing treatment by a health care provider; and

(6) the term "son or daughter" means a biological, adopted, or foster child, a stepchild, a legal ward, or a child of a person standing *in loco parentis*, who is —
(A) under 18 years of age; or
(B) 18 years of age or older and incapable of self-care because of a mental or physical disability.

5 U.S.C. § 6382. Leave requirement

(a)(1) Subject to section 6383, an employee shall be entitled to a total of 12 administrative workweeks of leave during any 12-month period for one or more of the following:
(A) Because of the birth of a son or daughter of the employee and in order to care for such son or daughter.
(B) Because of the placement of a son or daughter with the employee for adoption or foster care.
(C) In order to care for the spouse, or a son, daughter, or parent, of the employee, if such spouse, son, daughter, or parent has a serious health condition.
(D) Because of a serious health condition that makes the employee unable to perform the functions of the employee's position.
(2) The entitlement to leave under subparagraph (A) or (B) of paragraph (1) based on the birth or placement of a son or daughter shall expire at the end of the 12-month period beginning on the date of such birth or placement.

(b)(1) Leave under subparagraph (A) or (B) of subsection (a)(1) shall not be taken by an employee intermittently or on a reduced leave schedule unless the employee and the employing agency of the employee agree otherwise. Subject to paragraph (2), subsection (e)(2), and section 6383(b)(5), leave under subparagraph (C) or (D) of subsection (a)(1) may be taken intermittently or on a reduced leave schedule when medically necessary. In the case of an employee who takes leave intermittently or on a reduced leave schedule pursuant to this paragraph, any hours of leave so taken by such employee shall be subtracted from the total amount of leave remaining available to such employee under subsection (a), for purposes of the 12-month period involved, on an hour-for-hour basis.
(2) If an employee requests intermittent leave, or leave on a reduced leave schedule, under subparagraph (C) or (D) of subsection (a)(1), that is foreseeable based on planned medical treatment, the employing agency may require such employee to transfer temporarily to an available alternative position offered by the employing agency for which the employee is qualified and that —

(A) has equivalent pay and benefits; and

(B) better accommodates recurring periods of leave than the regular employment position of the employee.

(c) Except as provided in subsection (d), leave granted under subsection (a) shall be leave without pay.

(d) An employee may elect to substitute for leave under subparagraph (A), (B), (C), or (D) of subsection (a)(1) any of the employee's accrued or accumulated annual or sick leave under subchapter I for any part of the 12-week period of leave under such subsection, except that nothing in this subchapter shall require an employing agency to provide paid sick leave in any situation in which such employing agency would not normally provide any such paid leave.

(e)(1) In any case in which the necessity for leave under subparagraph (A) or (B) of subsection (a)(1) is foreseeable based on an expected birth or placement, the employee shall provide the employing agency with not less than 30 days' notice, before the date the leave is to begin, of the employee's intention to take leave under such subparagraph, except that if the date of the birth or placement requires leave to begin in less than 30 days, the employee shall provide such notice as is practicable.

(2) In any case in which the necessity for leave under subparagraph (C) or (D) of subsection (a)(1) is foreseeable based on planned medical treatment, the employee —

(A) shall make a reasonable effort to schedule the treatment so as not to disrupt unduly the operations of the employing agency, subject to the approval of the health care provider of the employee or the health care provider of the son, daughter, spouse, or parent of the employee, as appropriate; and

(B) shall provide the employing agency with not less than 30 days' notice, before the date the leave is to begin, of the employee's intention to take leave under such subparagraph, except that if the date of the treatment requires leave to begin in less than 30 days, the employee shall provide such notice as is practicable.

5 U.S.C. § 6383. Certification

(a) An employing agency may require that a request for leave under subparagraph (C) or (D) of section 6382(a)(1) be supported by certification issued by the health care provider of the employee or of the son, daughter, spouse, or parent of the employee, as appropriate. The employee shall provide, in a timely manner, a copy of such certification to the employing agency.

(b) A certification provided under subsection (a) shall be sufficient if it states —

(1) the date on which the serious health condition commenced;

(2) the probable duration of the condition;

(3) the appropriate medical facts within the knowledge of the health care provider regarding the condition;

(4)(A) for purposes of leave under section 6382(a)(1)(C), a statement that the employee is needed to care for the son, daughter, spouse, or parent, and an estimate of the amount of time that such employee is needed to care for such son, daughter, spouse, or parent; and

(B) for purposes of leave under section 6382(a)(1)(D), a statement that the employee is unable to perform the functions of the position of the employee; and

(5) in the case of certification for intermittent leave, or leave on a reduced leave schedule, for planned medical treatment, the dates on which such treatment is expected to be given and the duration of such treatment.

(c)(1) In any case in which the employing agency has reason to doubt the validity of the certification provided under subsection (a) for leave under subparagraph (C) or (D) of section 6382(a)(1), the employing agency may require, at the expense of the agency, that the employee obtain the opinion of a second health care provider designated or approved by the employing agency concerning any information certified under subsection (b) for such leave.

(2) Any health care provider designated or approved under paragraph (1) shall not be employed on a regular basis by the employing agency.

(d)(1) In any case in which the second opinion described in subsection (c) differs from the original certification provided under subsection (a), the employing agency may require, at the expense of the agency, that the employee obtain the opinion of a third health care provider designated or approved jointly by the employing agency and the employee concerning the information certified under subsection (b).

(2) The opinion of the third health care provider concerning the information certified under subsection (b) shall be considered to be final and shall be binding on the employing agency and the employee.

(e) The employing agency may require, at the expense of the agency, that the employee obtain subsequent recertifications on a reasonable basis.

5 U.S.C. § 6384. Employment and benefits protection

(a) Any employee who takes leave under section 6382 for the intended purpose of the leave shall be entitled, upon return from such leave —

(1) to be restored by the employing agency to the position held by the employee when the leave commenced; or

(2) to be restored to an equivalent position with equivalent benefits, pay, status, and other terms and conditions of employment.

(b) The taking of leave under section 6382 shall not result in the loss of any employment benefit accrued prior to the date on which the leave commenced.

(c) Except as otherwise provided by or under law, nothing in this section shall be construed to entitle any restored employee to —

(1) the accrual of any employment benefits during any period of leave; or

(2) any right, benefit, or position of employment other than any right, benefit, or position to which the employee would have been entitled had the employee not taken the leave.

(d) As a condition to restoration under subsection (a) for an employee who takes leave under section 6382(a)(1)(D), the employing agency may have a uniformly applied practice or policy that requires each such employee to receive certification from the health care provider of the employee that the employee is able to resume work.

(e) Nothing in this section shall be construed to prohibit an employing agency from requiring an employee on leave under section 6382 to report periodically to the employing agency on the status and intention of the employee to return to work.

5 U.S.C. § 6385. Prohibition of coercion

(a) An employee shall not directly or indirectly intimidate, threaten, or coerce, or attempt to intimidate, threaten, or coerce, any other employee for the purpose of interfering with the exercise of any rights which such other employee may have under this subchapter.

(b) For the purpose of this section —

(1) the term "intimidate, threaten, or coerce" includes promising to confer or conferring any benefit (such as appointment, promotion, or compensation), or taking or threatening to take any reprisal (such as deprivation of appointment, promotion, or compensation); and

(2) the term "employee" means any "employee", as defined by section 2105.

5 U.S.C. § 6386. Health insurance

An employee enrolled in a health benefits plan under chapter 89 [5 U.S.C. §8901 *et seq.*] who is placed in a leave status under section 6382 may elect to continue the health benefits enrollment of the employee while in such leave status and arrange to pay currently into the Employees Health Benefits Fund (described in section 8909), the appropriate employee contributions.

5 U.S.C. § 6387. Regulations

The Office of Personnel Management shall prescribe regulations necessary for the administration of this subchapter. The regulations prescribed under this subchapter shall, to the extent appropriate, be consistent with the regulations prescribed by the Secretary of Labor to carry out title I of the Family and Medical Leave Act of 1993.

APPENDIX C
FMLA REGULATIONS ISSUED BY THE
U.S. DEPARTMENT OF LABOR (DOL)
29 C.F.R. §§ 825.100–825.800

Subpart A: What is the Family and Medical Leave Act, and to whom does it apply?

Subpart C: **How do employees learn of their FMLA rights and obligations, and what can an employer require of an employee?**

SUBPART A
What is the Family and Medical Leave Act, and
to whom does it apply?

§ 825.100 What is the Family and Medical Leave Act?

(a) The Family and Medical Leave Act of 1993 (FMLA or Act) allows "eligible" employees of a covered employer to take job-protected, unpaid leave, or to substitute appropriate paid leave if the employee has earned or accrued it, for up to a total of 12 workweeks in any 12 months because of the birth of a child and to care for the newborn child, because of the placement of a child with the employee for adoption or foster care, because the employee is needed to care for a family member (child, spouse, or parent) with a serious health condition, or because the employee's own serious health condition makes the employee unable to perform the functions of his or her job (*see* § 825.306(b)(4)). In certain cases, this leave may be taken on an intermittent basis rather than all at once, or the employee may work a part-time schedule.

(b) An employee on FMLA leave is also entitled to have health benefits maintained while on leave as if the employee had continued to work instead of taking the leave. If an employee was paying all or part of the premium payments prior to leave, the employee would continue to pay his or her share during the leave period. The employer may recover its share only if the employee does not return to work for a reason other than the serious health condition of the employee or the employee's immediate family member, or another reason beyond the employee's control.

(c) An employee generally has a right to return to the same position or an equivalent position with equivalent pay, benefits and working conditions at the conclusion of the leave. The taking of FMLA leave cannot result in the loss of any benefit that accrued prior to the start of the leave.

(d) The employer has a right to 30 days advance notice from the employee where practicable. In addition, the employer may require an employee to submit certification from a health care provider to substantiate that the leave is due to the serious health condition of the employee or the employee's immediate family member. Failure to comply with these requirements may result in a delay in the start of FMLA leave. Pursuant to a uniformly applied policy, the employer may also require that an employee present a certification of fitness to return to work when the absence was caused by the employee's serious health condition (*see* § 825.311(c)). The employer may delay restoring the employee to employment without such certificate relating to the health condition which caused the employee's absence.

§ 825.101 What is the purpose of the Act?

(a) FMLA is intended to allow employees to balance their work and family life by taking reasonable unpaid leave for medical reasons, for the birth or adoption of a child, and for the care of a child, spouse, or parent who has a serious health condition. The Act is intended to balance the demands of the workplace with the needs of families, to promote the stability and economic security of families, and to promote national interests in preserving family integrity. It was intended that the Act accomplish these purposes in a manner that accommodates the legitimate interests of employers, and in a manner consistent with the Equal Protection Clause of the Fourteenth Amendment in minimizing the potential for employment discrimination on the basis of sex, while promoting equal employment opportunity for men and women.

(b) The enactment of FMLA was predicated on two fundamental concerns—the needs of the American workforce, and the development of high-performance organizations. Increasingly, America's children and elderly are dependent upon family members who must spend long hours at work. When a family emergency arises, requiring workers to attend to seriously-ill children or parents, or to newly-born or adopted infants, or even to their own serious illness, workers need reassurance that they will not be asked to choose between continuing their employment, and meeting their personal and family obligations or tending to vital needs at home.

(c) The FMLA is both intended and expected to benefit employers as well as their employees. A direct correlation exists between stability in the family and productivity in the workplace. FMLA will encourage the development of high-performance organizations. When workers can count on durable links to their workplace they are able to make their own full commitments to their jobs. The record of hearings on family and medical leave indicate the powerful productive advantages of stable workplace relationships, and the comparatively small costs of guaranteeing that those relationships will not be dissolved while workers attend to pressing family health obligations or their own serious illness.

§ 825.102 When was the Act effective?

(a) The Act became effective on August 5, 1993, for most employers. If a collective bargaining agreement was in effect on that date, the Act's effective date was delayed until February 5, 1994, or the date the agreement expired, whichever date occurred sooner. This delayed effective date was applicable only to employees covered by a collective bargaining agreement that was in effect on August 5, 1993, and not, for example, to employees outside the bargaining unit. Application of FMLA to collective bargaining agreements is discussed further in § 825.700(c).

(b) The period prior to the Act's effective date must be considered in determining employer coverage and employee eligibility. For example, as discussed further below, an employer with no collective bargaining agreements in effect as of August 5, 1993, must count employees/workweeks for calendar year 1992 and calendar year 1993. If 50 or more employees were employed during 20 or more workweeks in *either* 1992 or 1993 (through August 5, 1993), the employer was covered under FMLA on August 5, 1993. If not, the employer was not covered on August 5, 1993, but must continue to monitor employment levels each workweek remaining in 1993 and thereafter to determine if and when it might become covered.

§ 825.103 How did the Act affect leave in progress on, or taken before, the effective date of the Act?

(a) An eligible employee's right to take FMLA leave began on the date that the Act went into effect for the employer (*see* the discussion of differing effective dates for collective bargaining agreements in §§ 825.102(a) and 825.700(c)). Any leave taken prior to the Act's effective date may not be counted for purposes of FMLA. If leave qualifying as FMLA leave was underway prior to the effective date of the Act and continued after the Act's effective date, only that portion of leave taken on or after the Act's effective date may be counted against the employee's leave entitlement under the FMLA.

(b) If an employer-approved leave was underway when the Act took effect, no further notice would be required of the employee unless the employee requested an extension of the leave. For leave which commenced on the effective date or shortly thereafter, such notice must have been given which was practicable, considering the foreseeability of the need for leave and the effective date of the statute.

(c) Starting on the Act's effective date, an employee is entitled to FMLA leave if the reason for the leave is qualifying under the Act, even if the event occasioning the need for leave (*e.g.*, the birth of a child) occurred before the effective date (so long as any other requirements are satisfied).

§ 825.104 What employers are covered by the Act?

(a) An employer covered by FMLA is any person engaged in commerce or in any industry or activity affecting commerce, who employs 50 or more employees for each working day during each of 20 or more calendar workweeks in the current or preceding calendar year. Employers covered by FMLA also include any person acting, directly or indirectly, in the interest of a covered employer to any of the employees of the employer, any successor in interest of a covered employer, and any public agency. Public agencies are covered employers without regard to the number of employees employed. Public as well as private elementary and secondary schools are also covered employers without regard to the number of employees employed. (*See* § 825.600.)

(b) The terms "commerce" and "industry affecting commerce" are defined in accordance with section 501(1) and (3) of the Labor Management Relations Act of 1947 (LMRA) (29 U.S.C. 142 (1) and (3)), as set forth in the definitions at section 825.800 of this part. For purposes of the FMLA, employers who meet the 50-employee coverage test are deemed to be engaged in commerce or in an industry or activity affecting commerce.

(c) Normally the legal entity which employs the employee is the employer under FMLA. Applying this principle, a corporation is a single employer rather than its separate establishments or divisions.

(1) Where one corporation has an ownership interest in another corporation, it is a separate employer unless it meets the "joint employment" test discussed in § 825.106, or the "integrated employer" test contained in paragraph (c)(2) of this section.

(2) Separate entities will be deemed to be parts of a single employer for purposes of FMLA if they meet the "integrated employer" test. Where this test is met, the employees of all entities making up the integrated employer will be counted in determining employer coverage and employee eligibility. A determination of whether or not separate entities are an integrated employer is not determined by the application of any single criterion, but rather the entire relationship is to be reviewed in its totality. Factors considered in determining whether two or more entities are an integrated employer include:

(i) Common management;

(ii) Interrelation between operations;

(iii) Centralized control of labor relations; and

(iv) Degree of common ownership/financial control.

(d) An "employer" includes any person who acts directly or indirectly in the interest of an employer to any of the employer's employees. The definition of "employer" in section 3(d) of the Fair Labor Standards Act (FLSA), 29 U.S.C. 203(d), similarly includes any person acting directly or indirectly in the interest of an employer in relation to an employee. As under the FLSA, individuals such as corporate officers "acting in the interest of an employer" are individually liable for any violations of the requirements of FMLA.

§ 825.105 In determining whether an employer is covered by FMLA, what does it mean to employ 50 or more employees for each working day during each of 20 or more calendar workweeks in the current or preceding calendar year?

(a) The definition of "employ" for purposes of FMLA is taken from the Fair Labor Standards Act, § 3(g). The courts have made it clear that the employment relationship under the FLSA is broader than the traditional common law concept of master and servant. The difference between the employment relationship under the FLSA and that under the common law arises from the fact that the term "employ" as defined in the Act includes "to suffer or permit to work". The courts have indicated that, while "to permit" requires a more positive action than "to suffer", both terms imply much less positive action than required by the common law. Mere knowledge by an employer of work done for the employer by another is sufficient to create the employment relationship under the Act. The courts have said that there is no definition that solves all problems as to the limitations of the employer-employee relationship under the Act; and that determination of the relation cannot be based on "isolated factors" or upon a single characteristic or "technical concepts", but depends "upon the circumstances of the whole activity" including the underlying "economic reality." In general an employee, as distinguished from an independent contractor who is engaged in a business of his/her own, is one who "follows the usual path of an employee" and is dependent on the business which he/she serves.

(b) Any employee whose name appears on the employer's payroll will be considered employed each working day of the calendar week, and must be counted whether or not any compensation is received for the week. However, the FMLA applies only to employees who are employed within any State of the United States, the District of Columbia or any Territory or possession of the United States. Employees who are employed outside these areas are not counted for purposes of determining employer coverage or employee eligibility.

(c) Employees on paid or unpaid leave, including FMLA leave, leaves of absence, disciplinary suspension, *etc.*, are counted as long as the employer has a reasonable expectation that the employee will later return to active employment. If there is no employer/employee relationship (as when an employee is laid off, whether temporarily or permanently) such individual is not counted. Part-time employees, like full-time employees, are considered to be employed each working day of the calendar week, as long as they are maintained on the payroll.

(d) An employee who does not begin to work for an employer until after the first working day of a calendar week, or who terminates employment before the last working day of a calendar week, is not considered employed on each working day of that calendar week.

(e) A private employer is covered if it maintained 50 or more employees on the payroll during 20 or more calendar workweeks (not necessarily consecutive workweeks) in either the current or the preceding calendar year.

(f) Once a private employer meets the 50 employees/20 workweeks threshold, the employer remains covered until it reaches a future point where it no longer has employed 50 employees for 20 (nonconsecutive) workweeks in the current and preceding calendar year. For example, if an employer who met the 50 employees/20 workweeks test in the calendar year as of August 5, 1993, subsequently dropped below 50 employees before the end of 1993 and continued to employ fewer than 50 employees in all workweeks throughout calendar year 1994, the employer would continue to be covered throughout calendar year 1994 because it met the coverage criteria for 20 workweeks of the preceding (*i.e.*, 1993) calendar year.

§ 825.106 How is "joint employment" treated under FMLA?

(a) Where two or more businesses exercise some control over the work or working conditions of the employee, the businesses may be joint employers under FMLA. Joint employers may be separate and distinct entities with separate owners, managers and facilities. Where the employee performs work which simultaneously benefits two or more employers, or works for two or more employers at different times during the workweek, a joint employment relationship generally will be considered to exist in situations such as:

(1) Where there is an arrangement between employers to share an employee's services or to interchange employees;

(2) Where one employer acts directly or indirectly in the interest of the other employer in relation to the employee; or,

(3) Where the employers are not completely disassociated with respect to the employee's employment and may be deemed to share control of the employee, directly or indirectly, because one employer controls, is controlled by, or is under common control with the other employer.

(b) A determination of whether or not a joint employment relationship exists is not determined by the application of any single criterion, but rather the entire relationship is to be viewed in its totality. For example, joint employment will ordinarily be found to exist when a temporary or leasing agency supplies employees to a second employer.

(c) In joint employment relationships, only the primary employer is responsible for giving required notices to its employees, providing FMLA leave, and maintenance of health benefits. Factors considered in determining which is the "primary" employer include authority/responsibility to hire and fire, assign/place the employee, make payroll, and provide employment benefits. For employees of temporary help or leasing agencies, for example, the placement agency most commonly would be the primary employer.

(d) Employees jointly employed by two employers must be counted by both employers, whether or not maintained on one of the employer's payroll, in determining employer coverage and employee eligibility. For example, an employer who jointly employs 15 workers from a leasing or temporary help agency and 40 permanent workers is covered by FMLA. An employee on leave who is working for a secondary employer is considered employed by the secondary employer, and must be counted for coverage and eligibility purposes, as long as the employer has a reasonable expectation that that employee will return to employment with that employer.

(e) Job restoration is the primary responsibility of the primary employer. The secondary employer is responsible for accepting the employee returning from FMLA leave in place of the replacement employee if the secondary employer continues to utilize an employee from the temporary or leasing agency, and the agency chooses to place the employee with the secondary employer. A secondary employer is also responsible for compliance with the prohibited acts provisions with respect to its temporary/leased employees, whether or not the secondary employer is covered by FMLA (*see* § 825.220(a)). The prohibited acts include prohibitions against interfering with an employee's attempt to exercise rights under the Act, or discharging or discriminating against an employee for opposing a practice which is unlawful under FMLA. A covered secondary employer will be responsible for compliance with *all* the provisions of the FMLA with respect to its regular, permanent workforce.

§ 825.107 What is meant by "successor in interest"?

(a) For purposes of FMLA, in determining whether an employer is covered because it is a "successor in interest" to a covered employer, the factors used under Title VII of the Civil Rights Act and the Vietnam Era Veterans' Adjustment Act will be considered. However, unlike Title VII, whether the successor has notice of the employee's claim is not a consideration. Notice may be relevant, however, in determining successor liability for violations of the predecessor. The factors to be considered include:
  (1) Substantial continuity of the same business operations;
  (2) Use of the same plant;
  (3) Continuity of the work force;
  (4) Similarity of jobs and working conditions;
  (5) Similarity of supervisory personnel;
  (6) Similarity in machinery, equipment, and production methods;
  (7) Similarity of products or services; and
  (8) The ability of the predecessor to provide relief.

(b) A determination of whether or not a "successor in interest" exists is not determined by the application of any single criterion, but rather the entire circumstances are to be viewed in their totality.

(c) When an employer is a "successor in interest," employees' entitlements are the same as if the employment by the predecessor and successor were continuous employment by a single employer. For example, the successor, whether or not it meets FMLA coverage criteria, must grant leave for eligible employees who had provided appropriate notice to the predecessor, or continue leave begun while employed by the predecessor, including maintenance of group health benefits during the leave and job restoration at the conclusion of the leave. A successor which meets FMLA's coverage criteria must count periods of employment and hours worked for the predecessor for purposes of determining employee eligibility for FMLA leave.

§ 825.108 What is a "public agency"?

(a) An "employer" under FMLA includes any "public agency," as defined in section 3(x) of the Fair Labor Standards Act, 29 U.S.C. 203(x). Section 3(x) of the FLSA defines "public agency" as the government of the United States; the government of a State or political subdivision of a State; or an agency of the United States, a State, or a political subdivision of a State, or any interstate governmental agency. "State" is further defined in Section 3(c) of the FLSA to include any State of the United States, the District of Columbia, or any Territory or possession of the United States.

(b) The determination of whether an entity is a "public" agency, as distinguished from a private employer, is determined by whether the agency has taxing authority, or whether the chief administrative officer or board, *etc.*, is elected by the voters at-large or their appointment is subject to approval by an elected official.

(c)(1) A State or a political subdivision of a State constitutes a single public agency and, therefore, a single employer for purposes of determining employee eligibility. For example, a State is a single employer; a county is a single employer; a city or town is a single employer. Where there is any question about whether a public entity is a public agency, as distinguished from a part of another public agency, the U.S. Bureau of the Census' "Census of Governments" will be determinative, except for new entities formed since the most recent publication of the "Census." For new entities, the criteria used by the Bureau of Census will be used to determine whether an entity is a public agency or a part of another agency, including existence as an organized entity, governmental character, and substantial autonomy of the entity.

(2) The Census Bureau takes a census of governments at 5 year intervals. Volume I, Government Organization, contains the official counts of the number of State and local governments. It includes tabulations of governments by State, type of government, size, and county location. Also produced is a universe list of governmental units, classified according to type of government. Copies of Volume I, Government Organization, and subse-

quent volumes are available from the Superintendent of Documents, U.S. Government Printing Office, Washington, D.C., 20402, U.S. Department of Commerce District Offices, or can be found in Regional and selective depository libraries. For a list of all depository libraries, write to the Government Printing Office, 710 N. Capitol St., NW, Washington, D.C. 20402.

(d) All public agencies are covered by FMLA regardless of the number of employees; they are not subject to the coverage threshold of 50 employees carried on the payroll each day for 20 or more weeks in a year. However, employees of public agencies must meet all of the requirements of eligibility, including the requirement that the employer (*e.g.*, State) employ 50 employees at the worksite or within 75 miles.

§ 825.109 Are Federal agencies covered by these regulations?

(a) Most employees of the government of the United States, if they are covered by the FMLA, are covered under Title II of the FMLA (incorporated in Title V, Chapter 63, Subchapter 5 of the United States Code) which is administered by the U.S. Office of Personnel Management (OPM). OPM has separate regulations at 5 CFR Part 630, Subpart L. In addition, employees of the Senate and House of Representatives are covered by Title V of the FMLA.

(b) The Federal Executive Branch employees within the jurisdiction of these regulations include:

(1) Employees of the Postal Service;

(2) Employees of the Postal Rate Commission;

(3) A part-time employee who does not have an established regular tour of duty during the administrative workweek; and,

(4) An employee serving under an intermittent appointment or temporary appointment with a time limitation of one year or less.

(c) Employees of other Federal executive agencies are also covered by these regulations if they are not covered by Title II of FMLA.

(d) Employees of the legislative or judicial branch of the United States are covered by these regulations only if they are employed in a unit which has employees in the competitive service. Examples include employees of the Government Printing Office and the U.S. Tax Court.

(e) For employees covered by these regulations, the U.S. Government constitutes a single employer for purposes of determining employee eligibility. These employees must meet all of the requirements for eligibility, including the requirement that the Federal Government employ 50 employees at the worksite or within 75 miles.

§ 825.110 Which employees are "eligible" to take leave under FMLA?

(a) An "eligible employee" is an employee of a *covered* employer who:

(1) Has been employed by the employer for at least 12 months, and

(2) Has been employed for at least 1,250 hours of service during the 12-month period immediately preceding the commencement of the leave, and

(3) Is employed at a worksite where 50 or more employees are employed by the employer within 75 miles of that worksite. (*See* § 825.105(a) regarding employees who work outside the U.S.)

(b) The 12 months an employee must have been employed by the employer need not be consecutive months. If an employee is maintained on the payroll for any part of a week, including any periods of paid or unpaid leave (sick, vacation) during which other benefits or compensation are provided by the employer (*e.g.*, workers' compensation, group health plan benefits, *etc.*), the week counts as a week of employment. For purposes of determining whether intermittent/occasional/casual employment qualifies as "at least 12 months," 52 weeks is deemed to be equal to 12 months.

(c) Whether an employee has worked the minimum 1,250 hours of service is determined according to the principles established under the Fair Labor Standards Act (FLSA) for determining compensable hours of work (*see* 29 CFR Part 785). The determining factor is the number of hours an employee has worked for the employer within the meaning of the FLSA. The determination is not limited by methods of recordkeeping, or by compensation agreements that do not accurately reflect all of the hours an employee has worked for or been in service to the employer. Any accurate accounting of actual hours worked under FLSA's principles may be used. In the event an employer does not maintain an accurate record of hours worked by an employee, including for employees who are exempt from FLSA's requirement that a record be kept of their hours worked (*e.g.*, bona fide executive, administrative, and professional employees as defined in FLSA Regulations, 29 CFR Part 541), the employer has the burden of showing that the employee has not worked the requisite hours. In the event the employer is unable to meet this burden the employee is deemed to have met this test. *See* also § 825.500(f). For this purpose, full-time teachers (*see* § 825.800 for definition) of an elementary or secondary school system, or institution of higher education, or other educational establishment or institution are deemed to meet the 1,250 hour test. An employer must be able to clearly demonstrate that such an employee did not work 1,250 hours during the previous 12 months in order to claim that the employee is not "eligible" for FMLA leave.

(d) The determinations of whether an employee has worked for the employer for at least 1,250 hours in the past 12 months and has been employed by the employer for a total of at least 12 months must be made as of the date leave commences. If an employee notifies the employer of need for FMLA leave before the employee meets these eligibility criteria, the employer must either confirm the employee's eligibility based upon a projection that the employee will be eligible on the date leave would commence or must advise the employee when the eligibility requirement is met. If the employer confirms eligibility at the time the notice for leave is received, the employer may not subsequently challenge the employee's eligibility. In the latter case, if the employer does not advise the employee whether the employee is eligible as soon as practicable (*i.e.*, two business days absent extenuating circumstances) after the date employee eligibility is determined, the employee will have satisfied the notice requirements and the notice of leave is considered current and outstanding until the employer does advise. If the employer fails to advise the employee whether the employee is eligible prior to the date the requested leave is to commence, the employee will be deemed eligible. The employer may not, then, deny the leave. Where the employee does not give notice of the need for leave more than two business days prior to commencing leave, the employee will be deemed to be eligible if the employer fails to advise the employee that the employee is not eligible within two business days of receiving the employee's notice.

(e) The period prior to the FMLA's effective date must be considered in determining employee's eligibility.

(f) Whether 50 employees are employed within 75 miles to ascertain an employee's eligibility for FMLA benefits is determined when the employee gives notice of the need for leave. Whether the leave is to be taken at one time or on an intermittent or reduced leave schedule basis, once an employee is determined eligible in response to that notice of the need for leave, the employee's eligibility is not affected by any subsequent change in the number of employees employed at or within 75 miles of the employee's worksite, for that specific notice of the need for leave. Similarly, an employer may not terminate employee leave that has already started if the employee-count drops below 50. For example, if an employer employs 60 employees in August, but expects that the number of employees will drop to 40 in December, the employer must grant FMLA benefits to an otherwise eligible employee who gives notice of the need for leave in August for a period of leave to begin in December.

§ 825.111 In determining if an employee is "eligible" under FMLA, how is the determination made whether the employer employs 50 employees within 75 miles of the worksite where the employee needing leave is employed?

(a) Generally, a worksite can refer to either a single location or a group of contiguous locations. Structures which form a campus or industrial park, or separate facilities in proximity with one another, may be considered a single site of employment. On the other hand, there may be several single sites of employment within a single building, such as an office building, if separate employers conduct activities within the building. For example, an office building with 50 different businesses as tenants will contain 50 sites of employment. The offices of each employer will be considered separate sites of employment for purposes of FMLA. An employee's worksite under FMLA will ordinarily be the site the employee reports to or, if none, from which the employee's work is assigned.

(1) Separate buildings or areas which are not directly connected or in immediate proximity are a single worksite if they are in reasonable geographic proximity, are used for the same purpose, and share the same staff and equipment. For example, if an employer manages a number of warehouses in a metropolitan area but regularly shifts or rotates the same employees from one building to another, the multiple warehouses would be a single worksite.

(2) For employees with no fixed worksite, *e.g.*, construction workers, transportation workers (*e.g.*, truck drivers, seamen, pilots), salespersons, *etc.*, the "worksite" is the site to which they are assigned as their home base, from which their work is assigned, or to which they report. For example, if a construction company headquartered in New Jersey opened a construction site in Ohio, and set up a mobile trailer on the construction site as the company's on-site office, the construction site in Ohio would be the worksite for any employees hired locally who report to the mobile trailer/company office daily for work assignments, *etc.* If that construction company also sent personnel such as job superintendents, foremen, engineers, an office manager, *etc.*, from New Jersey to the job site in Ohio, those workers sent from New Jersey continue to have the headquarters in New Jersey as their "worksite." The workers who have New Jersey as their worksite would not be counted in determining eligibility of employees whose home base is the Ohio worksite, but would be counted in determining eligibility of employees whose home base is New Jersey. For transportation employees, their worksite is the terminal to which they are assigned, report for work, depart, and return after completion of a work assignment. For example, an airline pilot may work for an airline with headquarters in New York, but the pilot regularly reports for duty and originates or begins flights from the company's facilities located in an airport in Chicago and returns to Chicago at the completion of one or more flights to go off duty. The pilot's worksite is the facility in Chicago. An employee's personal residence is not a worksite in the case of employees such as salespersons who travel a sales territory and who generally leave to work and return from work to their personal residence, or employees who work at home, as under the new concept of flexiplace. Rather, their worksite is the office to which the report and from which assignments are made.

(3) For purposes of determining that employee's eligibility, when an employee is jointly employed by two or more employers (*see* § 825.106), the employee's worksite is the primary employer's office from which the employee is assigned or reports. The employee is also counted by the secondary employer to determine eligibility for the secondary employer's full-time or permanent employees.

(b) The 75-mile distance is measured by surface miles, using surface transportation over public streets, roads, highways and waterways, by the shortest route from the facility where the eligible employee needing leave is employed. Absent available surface transportation between worksites, the distance is measured by using the most frequently utilized mode of transportation (*e.g.*, airline miles).

(c) The determination of how many employees are employed within 75 miles of the worksite of an employee is based on the number of employees maintained on the payroll. Employees of educational institutions who are employed permanently or who are under contract are "maintained on the payroll" during any portion of the year when school is not in session. See § 825.105(c).

§ 825.112 Under what kinds of circumstances are employers required to grant family or medical leave?

(a) Employers covered by FMLA are required to grant leave to eligible employees:

(1) For birth of a son or daughter, and to care for the newborn child;

(2) For placement with the employee of a son or daughter for adoption or foster care;

(3) To care for the employee's spouse, son, daughter, or parent with a serious health condition; and

(4) Because of a serious health condition that makes the employee unable to perform the functions of the employee's job.

(b) The right to take leave under FMLA applies equally to male and female employees. A father, as well as a mother, can take family leave for the birth, placement for adoption or foster care of a child.

(c) Circumstances may require that FMLA leave begin before the actual date of birth of a child. An expectant mother may take FMLA leave pursuant to paragraph (a)(4) of this section before the birth of the child for prenatal care or if her condition makes her unable to work.

(d) Employers covered by FMLA are required to grant FMLA leave pursuant to paragraph (a)(2) of this section before the actual placement or adoption of a child if an absence from work is required for the placement for adoption or foster care to proceed. For example, the employee may be required to attend counselling sessions, appear in court, consult with his or her attorney or the doctor(s) representing the birth parent, or submit to a physical examination. The source of an adopted child (*e.g.*, whether from a licensed placement agency or otherwise) is not a factor in determining eligibility for leave for this purpose.

(e) Foster care is 24-hour care for children in substitution for, and away from, their parents or guardian. Such placement is made by or with the agreement of the State as a result of a voluntary agreement between the parent or guardian that the child be removed from the home, or pursuant to a judicial determination of the necessity for foster care, and involves agreement between the State and foster family that the foster family will take care of the child. Although foster care may be with relatives of the child, State action is involved in the removal of the child from parental custody.

(f) In situations where the employer/employee relationship has been interrupted, such as an employee who has been on layoff, the employee must be recalled or otherwise be re-employed before being eligible for FMLA leave. Under such circumstances, an eligible employee is immediately entitled to further FMLA leave for a qualifying reason.

(g) FMLA leave is available for treatment for substance abuse provided the conditions of § 825.114 are met. However, treatment for substance abuse does not prevent an employer from taking employment action against an employee. The employer may not take action against the employee because the employee has exercised his or her right to take FMLA leave for treatment. However, if the employer has an established policy, applied in a non discriminatory manner that has been communicated to all employees, that provides under certain circumstances an employee may be terminated for substance abuse, pursuant to that policy the employee may be terminated whether or not the employee is presently taking FMLA leave. An employee may also take FMLA leave to care for an immediate family member who is receiving treatment for substance abuse. The employer may not take action against an employee who is providing care for an immediate family member receiving treatment for substance abuse.

§ 825.113 What do "spouse," "parent," and "son or daughter" mean for purposes of an employee qualifying to take FMLA leave?

(a) Spouse means a husband or wife as defined or recognized under State law for purposes of marriage in the State where the employee resides, including common law marriage in States where it is recognized.

(b) Parent means a biological parent or an individual who stands or stood *in loco parentis* to an employee when the employee was a son or daughter as defined in (c) below. This term does not include parents "in law".

(c) Son or daughter means a biological, adopted, or foster child, a stepchild, a legal ward, or a child of a person standing *in loco parentis*, who is either under age 18, or age 18 or older and "incapable of self-care because of a mental or physical disability."

(1) "Incapable of self-care" means that the individual requires active assistance or supervision to provide daily self care in three or more of the "activities of daily living" (ADLs) or "instrumental activities of daily living" (IADLs). Activities of daily living include adaptive activities such as caring appropriately for one's grooming and hygiene, bathing, dressing and eating. Instrumental activities of daily living include cooking, cleaning, shopping, taking public transportation, paying bills, maintaining a residence, using telephones and directories, using a post office, *etc.*

(2) "Physical or mental disability" means a physical or mental impairment that substantially limits one or more of the major life activities of an individual. Regulations at 29 CFR § 1630.2(h), (i), and (j), issued by the Equal Employment Opportunity Commission under the Americans with Disabilities Act (ADA), 42 U.S.C. 12101 *et seq.*, define these terms.

(3) Persons who are *"in loco parentis"* include those with day-to-day responsibilities to care for and financially support a child or, in the case of an employee, who had such responsibility for the employee when the employee was a child. A biological or legal relationship is not necessary.

(d) For purposes of confirmation of family relationship, the employer may require the employee giving notice of the need for leave to provide reasonable documentation or statement of family relationship. This documentation may take the form of a simple statement from the employee, or a child's birth certificate, a court document, *etc.* The employer is entitled to examine documentation such as a birth certificate, *etc.*, but the employee is entitled to the return of the official document submitted for this purpose.

§ 825.114 What is a "serious health condition" entitling an employee to FMLA leave?

(a) For purposes of FMLA, "serious health condition" entitling an employee to FMLA leave means an illness, injury, impairment, or physical or mental condition that involves:

(1) *Inpatient care* (*i.e.*, an overnight stay) in a hospital, hospice, or residential medical care facility, including any period of incapacity (for purposes of this section, defined to mean inability to work, attend school or perform other regular daily activities due to the serious health condition, treatment therefor, or recovery therefrom), or any subsequent treatment in connection with such inpatient care; or

(2) *Continuing treatment* by a health care provider. A serious health condition involving continuing treatment by a health care provider includes any one or more of the following:

(i) A period of *incapacity* (*i.e.*, inability to work, attend school or perform other regular daily activities due to the serious health condition, treatment therefor, or recovery therefrom) of more than three consecutive calendar days, and any subsequent treatment or period of incapacity relating to the same condition, that also involves:

(A) Treatment two or more times by a health care provider, by a nurse or physician's assistant under direct supervision of a health care provider, or by a provider of health care services (*e.g.*, physical therapist) under orders of, or on referral by, a health care provider; or

(B) Treatment by a health care provider on at least one occasion which results in a regimen of continuing treatment under the supervision of the health care provider.

(ii) Any period of incapacity due to pregnancy, or for prenatal care.

(iii) Any period of incapacity or treatment for such incapacity due to a chronic serious health condition. A chronic serious health condition is one which:

(A) Requires periodic visits for treatment by a health care provider, or by a nurse or physician's assistant under direct supervision of a health care provider;

(B) Continues over an extended period of time (including recurring episodes of a single underlying condition); and

(C) May cause episodic rather than a continuing period of incapacity (*e.g.*, asthma, diabetes, epilepsy, *etc.*).

(iv) A period of incapacity which is permanent or long-term due to a condition for which treatment may not be effective. The employee or family member must be under the continuing supervision of, but need not be receiving active treatment by, a health care provider. Examples include Alzheimer's, a severe stroke, or the terminal stages of a disease.

(v) Any period of absence to receive multiple treatments (including any period of recovery therefrom) by a health care provider or by a provider of health care services under orders of, or on referral by, a health care provider, either for restorative surgery after an accident or other injury, or for a condition that would likely result in a period of incapacity of more than three consecutive calendar days in the absence of medical intervention or treatment, such as cancer (chemotherapy, radiation, *etc.*), severe arthritis (physical therapy), kidney disease (dialysis).

(b) Treatment for purposes of paragraph (a) of this section includes (but is not limited to) examinations to determine if a serious health condition exists and evaluations of the condition. Treatment does not include routine physical examinations, eye examinations, or dental examinations. Under paragraph (a)(2)(i)(B), a regimen of continuing treatment includes, for example, a course of prescription medication (*e.g.*, an antibiotic) or therapy requiring special equipment to resolve or alleviate the health condition (*e.g.*, oxygen). A regimen of continuing treatment that includes the taking of over-the-counter medications such as aspirin, antihistamines, or salves; or bed-rest, drinking fluids, exercise, and other similar activities that can be initiated without a visit to a health care provider, is not, by itself, sufficient to constitute a regimen of continuing treatment for purposes of FMLA leave.

(c) Conditions for which cosmetic treatments are administered (such as most treatments for acne or plastic surgery) are not "serious health conditions" unless inpatient hospital care is required or unless complications develop. Ordinarily, unless complications arise, the common cold, the flu, ear aches, upset stomach, minor ulcers, headaches other than migraine, routine dental or orthodontia problems, periodontal disease, *etc.*, are examples of conditions that do not meet the definition of a serious health condition and do not qualify for FMLA leave. Restorative dental or plastic surgery after an injury or removal of cancerous growths are serious health conditions provided all the other conditions of this regulation are met. Mental illness resulting from stress or allergies may be serious health conditions, but only if all the conditions of this section are met.

(d) Substance abuse may be a serious health condition if the conditions of this section are met. However, FMLA leave may only be taken for treatment for substance abuse by a health care provider or by a provider of health care services on referral by a health care provider. On the other hand, absence because of the employee's use of the substance, rather than for treatment, does not qualify for FMLA leave.

(e) Absences attributable to incapacity under paragraphs (a)(2) (ii) or (iii) qualify for FMLA leave even though the employee or the immediate family member does not receive treatment from a health care provider during the absence, and even if the absence does not last more than three days. For example, an employee with asthma may be unable to report for work due to the onset of an asthma attack or because the employee's health care provider has advised the employee to stay home when the pollen count exceeds a certain level. An employee who is pregnant may be unable to report to work because of severe morning sickness.

§ 825.115 What does it mean that "the employee is unable to perform the functions of the position of the employee"?

An employee is "unable to perform the functions of the position" where the health care provider finds that the employee is unable to work at all or is unable to perform any one of the essential functions of the employee's position within the meaning of the Americans with Disabilities Act (ADA), 42 USC 12101 *et seq.*, and the regulations at 29 CFR § 1630.2(n). An employee who must be absent from work to receive medical treatment for a serious health condition is considered to be unable to perform the essential functions of the position during the absence for treatment. An employer has the option, in requiring certification from a health care provider, to provide a statement of the essential functions of the employee's position for the health care provider to review. For purposes of FMLA, the essential functions of the employee's position are to be determined with reference to the position the employee held at the time notice is given or leave commenced, whichever is earlier.

§ 825.116 What does it mean that an employee is "needed to care for" a family member?

(a) The medical certification provision that an employee is "needed to care for" a family member encompasses both physical and psychological care. It includes situations where, for example, because of a serious health condition, the family member is unable to care for his or her own basic medical, hygienic, or nutritional needs or safety, or is unable to transport himself or herself to the doctor, *etc.* The term also includes providing psychological comfort and reassurance which would be beneficial to a child, spouse or parent with a serious health condition who is receiving inpatient or home care.

(b) The term also includes situations where the employee may be needed to fill in for others who are caring for the family member, or to make arrangements for changes in care, such as transfer to a nursing home.

(c) An employee's intermittent leave or a reduced leave schedule necessary to care for a family member includes not only a situation where the family member's condition itself is intermittent, but also where the employee is only needed intermittently-such as where other care is normally available, or care responsibilities are shared with another member of the family or a third party.

§ 825.117 For an employee seeking intermittent FMLA leave or leave on a reduced leave schedule, what is meant by "the medical necessity for" such leave?

For intermittent leave or leave on a reduced leave schedule, there must be a medical need for leave (as distinguished from voluntary treatments and procedures) and it must be that such medical need can be best accommodated through an intermittent or reduced leave schedule. The treatment regimen and other information described in the certification of a serious health condition (*see* § 825.306) meets the requirement for certification of the medical necessity of intermittent leave or leave on a reduced leave schedule. Employees needing intermittent FMLA leave or leave on a reduced leave schedule must attempt to schedule their leave so as not to disrupt the employer's operations. In addition, an employer may assign an employee to an alternative position with equivalent pay and benefits that better accommodates the employee's intermittent or reduced leave schedule.

§ 825.118 What is a "health care provider"?

(a) The Act defines "health care provider" as:

(1) A doctor of medicine or osteopathy who is authorized to practice medicine or surgery (as appropriate) by the State in which the doctor practices; or

(2) Any other person determined by the Secretary to be capable of providing health care services.

(b) Others "capable of providing health care services" include only:

(1) Podiatrists, dentists, clinical psychologists, optometrists, and chiropractors (limited to treatment consisting of manual manipulation of the spine to correct a subluxation as demonstrated by X-ray to exist) authorized to practice in the State and performing within the scope of their practice as defined under State law;

(2) Nurse practitioners, nurse-midwives and clinical social workers who are authorized to practice under State law and who are performing within the scope of their practice as defined under State law;

(3) Christian Science practitioners listed with the First Church of Christ, Scientist in Boston, Massachusetts. Where an employee or family member is receiving treatment from a Christian Science practitioner, an employee may not object to any requirement from an employer that the employee or family member submit to examination (though not treatment) to obtain a second or third certification from a health care provider other than a Christian Science practitioner except as otherwise provided under applicable State or local law or collective bargaining agreement.

(4) Any health care provider from whom an employer or the employer's group health plan's benefits manager will accept certification of the existence of a serious health condition to substantiate a claim for benefits; and

(5) A health care provider listed above who practices in a country other than the United States, who is authorized to practice in accordance with the law of that country, and who is performing within the scope of his or her practice as defined under such law.

(c) The phrase "authorized to practice in the State" as used in this section means that the provider must be authorized to diagnose and treat physical or mental health conditions without supervision by a doctor or other health care provider.

SUBPART B
What leave is an employee entitled to take under the Family and Medical Leave Act?

§ 825.200 How much leave may an employee take?

(a) An eligible employee's FMLA leave entitlement is limited to a total of 12 workweeks of leave during any 12-month period for any one, or more, of the following reasons:

(1) The birth of the employee's son or daughter, and to care for the new-born child;

(2) The placement with the employee of a son or daughter for adoption or foster care, and to care for the newly placed child;

(3) To care for the employee's spouse, son, daughter, or parent with a serious health condition; and,

(4) Because of a serious health condition that makes the employee unable to perform one or more of the essential functions of his or her job.

(b) An employer is permitted to choose any one of the following methods for determining the "12-month period" in which the 12 weeks of leave entitlement occurs:

(1) The calendar year;

(2) Any fixed 12-month "leave year," such as a fiscal year, a year required by State law, or a year starting on an employee's "anniversary" date;

(3) The 12-month period measured forward from the date any employee's first FMLA leave begins; or,

(4) A "rolling" 12-month period measured backward from the date an employee uses any FMLA leave (except that such measure may not extend back before August 5, 1993).

(c) Under methods in paragraphs (b)(1) and (b)(2) of this section an employee would be entitled to up to 12 weeks of FMLA leave at any time in the fixed 12-month period selected. An employee could, therefore, take 12 weeks of leave at the end of the year and 12 weeks at the beginning of the following year. Under the method in paragraph (b)(3) of this section, an employee would be entitled to 12 weeks of leave during the year beginning on the first date FMLA leave is taken; the next 12-month period would begin the first time FMLA leave is taken after completion of any previous 12-month period. Under the method in paragraph (b)(4) of this section, the "rolling" 12-month period, each time an employee takes FMLA leave the remaining leave entitlement would be any balance of the 12 weeks which has not been used during the immediately preceding 12 months. For example, if an employee has taken eight weeks of leave during the past 12 months, an additional four weeks of leave could be taken. If an employee used four weeks beginning February 1, 1994, four weeks beginning June 1, 1994, and four weeks beginning December 1, 1994, the employee would not be entitled to any additional leave until February 1, 1995. However, beginning on February 1, 1995, the employee would be entitled to four weeks of leave, on June 1 the employee would be entitled to an additional four weeks, *etc.*

(d)(1) Employers will be allowed to choose any one of the alternatives in paragraph (b) of this section provided the alternative chosen is applied consistently and uniformly to all employees. An employer wishing to change to another alternative is required to give at least 60 days notice to all employees, and the transition must take place in such a way that the employees retain the full benefit of 12 weeks of leave under whichever method affords the greatest benefit to the employee. Under no circumstances may a new method be implemented in order to avoid the Act's leave requirements.

(2) An exception to this required uniformity would apply in the case of a multi-State employer who has eligible employees in a State which has a family and medical leave statute. The State may require a single method of determining the period during which use of the leave entitlement is measured. This method may conflict with the method chosen by the employer to determine "any 12 months" for purposes of the Federal statute. The employer may comply with the State provision for all employees employed within that State, and uniformly use another method provided by this regulation for all other employees.

(e) If an employer fails to select one of the options in paragraph (b) of this section for measuring the 12-month period, the option that provides the most beneficial outcome for the employee will be used. The employer may subsequently select an option only by providing the 60-day notice to all employees of the option the employer intends to implement. During the running of the 60-day period any other employee who needs FMLA leave may use the option providing the most beneficial outcome to that employee. At the conclusion of the 60-day period the employer may implement the selected option.

(f) For purposes of determining the amount of leave used by an employee, the fact that a holiday may occur within the week taken as FMLA leave has no effect; the week is counted as a week of FMLA leave. However, if for some reason the employer's business activity has temporarily ceased and employees generally are not expected to report for work for one or more weeks (*e.g.*, a school closing two weeks for the Christmas/New Year holiday or the summer vacation or an employer closing the plant for retooling or repairs), the days the employer's activities have ceased do *not* count against the employee's FMLA leave entitlement. Methods for determining an employee's 12-week leave entitlement are also described in § 825.205.

§ 825.201 If leave is taken for the birth of a child, or for placement of a child for adoption or foster care, when must the leave be concluded?

An employee's entitlement to leave for a birth or placement for adoption or foster care expires at the end of the 12-month period beginning on the date of the birth or placement, unless state law allows, or the employer permits, leave to be taken for a longer period. Any such FMLA leave must be concluded within this one-year period. However, *see* § 825.701 regarding non-FMLA leave which may be available under applicable State laws.

§ 825.202 How much leave may a husband and wife take if they are employed by the same employer?

(a) A husband and wife who are eligible for FMLA leave and are employed by the same covered employer may be limited to a combined total of 12 weeks of leave during any 12-month period if the leave is taken:

(1) for birth of the employee's son or daughter or to care for the child after birth;

(2) for placement of a son or daughter with the employee for adoption or foster care, or to care for the child after placement; or

(3) to care for the employee's parent with a serious health condition.

(b) This limitation on the total weeks of leave applies to leave taken for the reasons specified in paragraph (a) of this section as long as a husband and wife are employed by the "same employer." It would apply, for example, even though the spouses are employed at two different worksites of an employer located more than 75 miles from each other, or by two different operating divisions of the same company. On the other hand, if one spouse is ineligible for FMLA leave, the other spouse would be entitled to a full 12 weeks of FMLA leave.

(c) Where the husband and wife both use a portion of the total 12-week FMLA leave entitlement for one of the purposes in paragraph (a) of this section, the husband and wife would each be entitled to the difference between the amount he or she has taken individually and 12 weeks for FMLA leave for a purpose other than those contained in paragraph (a) of this section. For example, if each spouse took 6 weeks of leave to care for a healthy, newborn child, each could use an additional 6 weeks due to his or her own serious health condition or to care for a child with a serious health condition. Note, too, that many State pregnancy disability laws specify a period of disability either before or after the birth of a child; such periods would also be considered FMLA leave for a serious health condition of the mother, and would not be subject to the combined limit.

§ 825.203 Does FMLA leave have to be taken all at once, or can it be taken in parts?

(a) FMLA leave may be taken "intermittently or on a reduced leave schedule" under certain circumstances. Intermittent leave is FMLA leave taken in separate blocks of time due to a single qualifying reason. A reduced leave schedule is a leave schedule that reduces an employee's usual number of working hours per workweek, or hours per workday. A reduced leave schedule is a change in the employee's schedule for a period of time, normally from full-time to part-time.

(b) When leave is taken after the birth or placement of a child for adoption or foster care, an employee may take leave intermittently or on a reduced leave schedule only if the employer agrees. Such a schedule reduction might occur, for example, where an employee, with the employer's agreement, works part time after the birth of a child, or takes leave in several segments. The employer's agreement is not required, however, for leave during which the mother has a serious health condition in connection with the birth of her child or if the newborn child has a serious health condition.

(c) Leave may be taken intermittently or on a reduced leave schedule when medically necessary for planned and/or unanticipated medical treatment of a related serious health condition by or under the supervision of a health care provider, or for recovery from treatment or recovery from a serious health condition. It may also be taken to provide care or psychological comfort to an immediate family member with a serious health condition.

(1) Intermittent leave may be taken for a serious health condition which requires treatment by a health care provider periodically, rather than for one continuous period of time, and may include leave of periods from an hour or more to several weeks. Examples of intermittent leave would include leave taken on an occasional basis for medical appointments, or leave taken several days at a time spread over a period of six months, such as for chemotherapy. A pregnant employee may take leave intermittently for prenatal examinations or for her own condition, such as for periods of severe morning sickness. An example of an employee taking leave on a reduced leave schedule is an employee who is recovering from a serious health condition and is not strong enough to work a full-time schedule.

(2) Intermittent or reduced schedule leave may be taken for absences where the employee or family member is incapacitated or unable to perform the essential functions of the position because of a chronic serious health condition even if he or she does not receive treatment by a health care provider.

(d) There is no limit on the size of an increment of leave when an employee takes intermittent leave or leave on a reduced leave schedule. However, an employer may limit leave increments to the shortest period of time that the employer's payroll system uses to account for absences or use of leave, provided it is one hour or less. For example, an employee might take two hours off for a medical appointment, or might work a reduced day of four hours over a period of several weeks while recuperating from an illness. An employee may not be required to take more FMLA leave than necessary to address the circumstance that precipitated the need for the leave, except as provided in §§ 825.601 and 825.602.

§ 825.204 May an employer transfer an employee to an "alternative position" in order to accommodate intermittent leave or a reduced leave schedule?

(a) If an employee needs intermittent leave or leave on a reduced leave schedule that is foreseeable based on planned medical treatment for the employee or a family member, including during a period of recovery from a serious health condition, or if the employer agrees to permit intermittent or reduced schedule leave for the birth of a child or for placement of a child for adoption or foster care, the employer may require the employee to transfer temporarily, during the period the intermittent or reduced leave schedule is required, to an available alternative position for which the employee is qualified and which better accommodates recurring periods of leave than does the employee's regular position. *See* § 825.601 for special rules applicable to instructional employees of schools.

(b) Transfer to an alternative position may require compliance with any applicable collective bargaining agreement, federal law (such as the Americans with Disabilities Act), and State law. Transfer to an alternative position may include altering an existing job to better accommodate the employee's need for intermittent or reduced leave.

(c) The alternative position must have equivalent pay and benefits. An alternative position for these purposes does not have to have equivalent duties. The employer may increase the pay and benefits of an existing alternative position, so as to make them equivalent to the pay and benefits of the employee's regular job. The employer may also transfer the employee to a part-time job with the same hourly rate of pay and benefits, provided the employee is not required to take more leave than is medically necessary. For example, an employee desiring to take leave in increments of four hours per day could be transferred to a half-time job, or could remain in the employee's same job on a part-time schedule, paying the same hourly rate as the employee's previous job and enjoying the same benefits. The employer may not eliminate benefits which otherwise would not be provided to part-time employees; however, an employer may proportionately reduce benefits such as vacation leave where an employer's normal practice is to base such benefits on the number of hours worked.

(d) An employer may not transfer the employee to an alternative position in order to discourage the employee from taking leave or otherwise work a hardship on the employee. For example, a white collar employee may not be assigned to perform laborer's work; an employee working the day shift may not be reassigned to the graveyard shift; an employee working in the headquarters facility may not be reassigned to a branch a significant distance away from the employee's normal job location. Any such attempt on the part of the employer to make such a transfer will be held to be contrary to the prohibited acts of the FMLA.

(e) When an employee who is taking leave intermittently or on a reduced leave schedule and has been transferred to an alternative position, no longer needs to continue on leave and is able to return to full-time work, the employee must be placed in the same or equivalent job as the job he/she left when the leave commenced. An employee may not be required to take more leave than necessary to address the circumstance that precipitated the need for leave.

§ 825.205 How does one determine the amount of leave used where an employee takes leave intermittently or on a reduced leave schedule?

(a) If an employee takes leave on an intermittent or reduced leave schedule, only the amount of leave actually taken may be counted toward the 12 weeks of leave to which an employee is entitled. For example, if an employee who normally works five days a week takes off one day, the employee would use 1/5 of a week of FMLA leave. Similarly, if a full-time employee who normally works 8-hour days works 4-hour days under a reduced leave schedule, the employee would use 1/2 week of FMLA leave each week.

(b) Where an employee normally works a part-time schedule or variable hours, the amount of leave to which an employee is entitled is determined on a pro rata or proportional basis by comparing the new schedule with the employee's normal schedule. For example, if an employee who normally works 30 hours per weekworks only 20 hours a week under a reduced leave schedule, the employee's ten hours of leave would constitute one-third of a week of FMLA leave for each week the employee works the reduced leave schedule.

(c) If an employer has made a permanent or long-term change in the employee's schedule (for reasons other than FMLA, and prior to the notice of need for FMLA leave), the hours worked under the new schedule are to be used for making this calculation.

(d) If an employee's schedule varies from week to week, a weekly average of the hours worked over the 12 weeks prior to the beginning of the leave period would be used for calculating the employee's normal workweek.

§ 825.206 May an employer deduct hourly amounts from an employee's salary, when providing unpaid leave under FMLA, without affecting the employee's qualification for exemption as an executive, administrative, or professional employee, or when utilizing the fluctuating workweek method for payment of overtime, under the Fair Labor Standards Act?

(a) Leave taken under FMLA may be unpaid. If an employee is otherwise exempt from minimum wage and overtime requirements of the Fair Labor Standards Act (FLSA) as a salaried executive, administrative, or professional employee (under regulations issued by the Secretary), 29 CFR Part 541, providing unpaid FMLA-qualifying leave to such an employee will not cause the employee to lose the FLSA exemption. This means that under regulations currently in effect, where an employee meets the specified duties test, is paid on a salary basis, and is paid a salary of at least the amount specified in the regulations, the employer may make deductions from the employee's salary for any hours taken as intermittent or reduced FMLA leave within a workweek, without affecting the exempt status of the employee. The fact that an employer provides FMLA leave, whether paid or unpaid, and maintains records required by this part regarding FMLA leave, will not be relevant to the determination whether an employee is exempt within the meaning of 29 CFR Part 541.

(b) For an employee paid in accordance with the fluctuating workweek method of payment for overtime (*see* 29 CFR 778.114), the employer, *during the period* in which intermittent or reduced schedule FMLA leave is scheduled to be taken, may compensate an employee on an hourly basis and pay only for the hours the employee works, including time and one-half the employee's regular rate for overtime hours. The change to payment on an hourly basis would include the entire period during which the employee is taking intermittent leave, including weeks in which no leave is taken. The hourly rate shall be determined by dividing the employee's weekly salary by the employee's normal or average schedule of hours worked during weeks in which FMLA leave is not being taken. If an employer chooses to follow this exception from the fluctuating workweek method of payment, the employer must do so uniformly, with respect to all employees paid on a fluctuating workweek basis for whom FMLA leave is taken on an intermittent or reduced leave schedule basis. If an employer does not elect to convert the employee's compensation to hourly pay, no deduction may be taken for FMLA leave absences. Once the need for intermittent or reduced scheduled leave is over, the employee may be restored to payment on a fluctuating work week basis.

(c) This special exception to the "salary basis" requirements of the FLSA exemption or fluctuating workweek payment requirements applies only to employees of covered employers who are eligible for FMLA leave, and to leave which qualifies as (one of the four types of) FMLA leave. Hourly or other deductions which are not in accordance with 29 CFR Part 541 or 29 CFR § 778.114 may *not* be taken, for example, from the salary of an employee who works for an employer with fewer than 50 employees, or where the employee has not worked long enough to be eligible for FMLA leave without potentially affecting the employee's eligibility for exemption. Nor may deductions which are not permitted by 29 CFR Part 541 or 29 CFR § 778.114 be taken from such an employee's salary for any leave which does not qualify as FMLA leave, for example, deductions from an employee's pay for leave required under State law or under an employer's policy or practice for a reason which does not qualify as FMLA leave, *e.g.*, leave to care for a grandparent or for a medical condition which does not qualify as a serious health condition; or for leave which is more generous than provided by FMLA, such as leave in excess of 12 weeks in a year. Employers may comply with State law or the employer's own policy/practice under these circumstances and maintain the employee's eligibility for exemption or for the fluctuating workweek method of pay by not taking hourly deductions from the employee's pay, in accordance with FLSA requirements, or may take such deductions, treating the employee as an "hourly" employee and pay overtime premium pay for hours worked over 40 in a workweek.

§ 825.207 Is FMLA leave paid or unpaid?

(a) Generally, FMLA leave is unpaid. However, under the circumstances described in this section, FMLA permits an eligible employee to choose to substitute paid leave for FMLA leave. If an employee does not choose to substitute accrued paid leave, the employer may require the employee to substitute accrued paid leave for FMLA leave.

(b) Where an employee has earned or accrued paid vacation, personal or family leave, that paid leave may be substituted for all or part of any (otherwise) unpaid FMLA leave relating to birth, placement of a child for adoption or foster care, or care for a spouse, child or parent who has a serious health condition. The term "family leave" as used in FMLA refers to paid leave provided by the employer covering the particular circumstances for which the employee seeks leave for either the birth of a child and to care for such child, placement of a child for adoption or foster care, or care for a spouse, child or parent with a serious health condition. For example, if the employer's leave plan allows use of family leave to care for a child but not for a parent, the employer is not required to allow accrued family leave to be substituted for FMLA leave used to care for a parent.

(c) Substitution of paid accrued vacation, personal, or medical/sick leave may be made for any (otherwise) unpaid FMLA leave needed to care for a family member or the employee's own serious health condition. Substitution of paid sick/medical leave may be elected to the extent the circumstances meet the employer's usual requirements for the use of sick/medical leave. An employer is not required to allow substitution of paid sick or medical leave for unpaid FMLA leave "in any situation" where the employer's uniform policy would not normally allow such paid leave. An employee, therefore, has a right to substitute paid medical/sick leave to care for a seriously ill family member only if the employer's leave plan allows paid leave to be used for that purpose. Similarly, an employee does not have a right to substitute paid medical/sick leave for a serious health condition which is not covered by the employer's leave plan.

(d)(1) Disability leave for the birth of a child would be considered FMLA leave for a serious health condition and counted in the 12 weeks of leave permitted under FMLA. Because the leave pursuant to a temporary disability benefit plan is not unpaid, the provision for substitution of paid leave is inapplicable. However, the employer may designate the leave as FMLA leave and count the leave as running concurrently for purposes of both the benefit plan and the FMLA leave entitlement. If the requirements to qualify for payments pursuant to the employer's temporary disability plan are more stringent than those of FMLA, the employee must meet the more stringent requirements of the plan, or may choose not to meet the requirements of the plan and instead receive no payments from the plan and use unpaid FMLA leave or substitute available accrued paid leave.

(2) The Act provides that a serious health condition may result from injury to the employee "on or off" the job. If the employer designates the leave as FMLA leave in accordance with § 825.208, the employee's FMLA 12-week leave entitlement may run concurrently with a workers' compensation absence when the injury is one that meets the criteria for a serious health condition. As the workers' compensation absence is not unpaid leave, the provision for substitution of the employee's accrued paid leave is not applicable. However, if the health care provider treating the employee for the workers' compensation injury certifies the employee is able to return to a "light duty job" but is unable to return to the same or equivalent job, the employee may decline the employer's offer of a "light duty job". As a result the employee may lose workers' compensation payments, but is entitled to remain on unpaid FMLA leave until the 12-week entitlement is exhausted. As of the date workers' compensation benefits cease, the substitution provision becomes applicable and either the employee may elect or the employer may require the use of accrued paid leave. *See also* §§ 825.210(f), 825.216(d), 825.220(d), 825.307(a)(1) and 825.702(d) (1) and (2) regarding the relationship between workers' compensation absences and FMLA leave.

(e) Paid vacation or personal leave, including leave earned or accrued under plans allowing "paid time off," may be substituted, at either the employee's or the employer's option, for any qualified FMLA leave. No limitations may be placed by the employer on substitution of paid vacation or personal leave for these purposes.

(f) If neither the employee nor the employer elects to substitute paid leave for unpaid FMLA leave under the above conditions and circumstances, the employee will remain entitled to all the paid leave which is earned or accrued under the terms of the employer's plan.

(g) If an employee uses paid leave under circumstances which do not qualify as FMLA leave, the leave will not count against the 12 weeks of FMLA leave to which the employee is entitled. For example, paid sick leave used for a medical condition which is not a serious health condition does not count against the 12 weeks of FMLA leave entitlement.

(h) When an employee or employer elects to substitute paid leave (of any type) for unpaid FMLA leave under circumstances permitted by these regulations, and the employer's procedural requirements for taking that kind of leave are less stringent than the requirements of FMLA (*e.g.*, notice or certification requirements), only the less stringent requirements may be imposed. An employee who complies with an employer's less stringent leave plan requirements in such cases may not have leave for an FMLA purpose delayed or denied on the grounds that the employee has not complied with stricter requirements of FMLA. However, where accrued paid vacation or personal leave is substituted for unpaid FMLA leave for a serious health condition, an employee may be required to comply with any less stringent medical certification requirements of the employer's sick leave program. *See* §§ 825.302(g), 825.305(e) and 825.306(c).

(i) Section 7(o) of the Fair Labor Standards Act (FLSA) permits public employers under prescribed circumstances to substitute compensatory time off accrued at one and one-half hours for each overtime hour worked in lieu of paying cash to an employee when the employee works overtime hours as prescribed by the Act. There are limits to the amounts of hours of compensatory time an employee may accumulate depending upon whether the employee works in fire protection or law enforcement (480 hours) or elsewhere for a public agency (240 hours). Compensatory time off is not a form of accrued paid leave that an employer may require the employee to substitute for unpaid FMLA leave. The employee may request to use his/her balance of compensatory time for an FMLA reason. If the employer permits the accrual to be used in compliance with regulations, 29 CFR 553.25, the absence which is paid from the employee's accrued compensatory time "account" may not be counted against the employee's FMLA leave entitlement.

§ 825.208 Under what circumstances may an employer designate leave, paid or unpaid, as FMLA leave and, as a result, count it against the employee's total FMLA leave entitlement?

(a) In all circumstances, it is the employer's responsibility to designate leave, paid or unpaid, as FMLA-qualifying, and to give notice of the designation to the employee as provided in this section. In the case of intermittent leave or leave on a reduced schedule, only one such notice is required unless the circumstances regarding the leave have changed. The employer's designation decision must be based only on information received from the employee or the employee's spokesperson (*e.g.*, if the employee is incapacitated, the employee's spouse, adult child, parent, doctor, *etc.*, may provide notice to the employer of the need to take FMLA leave). In any circumstance where the employer does not have sufficient information about the reason for an employee's use of paid leavc, the employer should inquire further of the employee or the spokesperson to ascertain whether the paid leave is potentially FMLA-qualifying.

(1) An employee giving notice of the need for unpaid FMLA leave must explain the reasons for the needed leave so as to allow the employer to determine that the leave qualifies under the Act. If the employee fails to explain the reasons, leave may be denied. In many cases, in explaining the reasons for a request to use paid leave, especially when the need for the leave was unexpected or unforeseen, an employee will provide sufficient information for the employer to designate the paid leave as FMLA leave. An employee using accrued paid leave, especially vacation or personal leave, may in some cases not spontaneously explain the reasons or their plans for using their accrued leave.

(2) As noted in § 825.302(c), an employee giving notice of the need for unpaid FMLA leave does not need to expressly assert rights under the Act or even mention the FMLA to meet his or her obligation to provide notice, though the employee would need to state a qualifying reason for the needed leave. An employee requesting or notifying the employer of an intent to use accrued paid leave, even if for a purpose covered by FMLA, would not need to assert such right either. However, if an employee requesting to use paid leave for an FMLA-qualifying purpose does not explain the reason for the leave-consistent with the employer's established policy or practice-and the employer denies the employee's request, the employee will need to provide sufficient information to establish an FMLA-qualifying reason for the needed leave so that the employer is aware of the employee's entitlement (*i.e.*, that the leave may not be denied) and, then, may designate that the paid leave be appropriately counted against (substituted for) the employee's 12-week entitlement. Similarly, an employee using accrued paid vacation leave who seeks an extension of unpaid leave for an FMLA-qualifying purpose will need to state the reason. If this is due to an event which occurred during the period of paid leave, the employer may count the leave used after the FMLA-qualifying event against the employee's 12-week entitlement.

(b)(1) Once the employer has acquired knowledge that the leave is being taken for an FMLA required reason, the employer must promptly (within two business days absent extenuating circumstances) notify the employee that the paid leave is designated and will be counted as FMLA leave. If there is a dispute between an employer and an employee as to whether paid leave qualifies as FMLA leave, it should be resolved through discussions between the employee and the employer. Such discussions and the decision must be documented.

(2) The employer's notice to the employee that the leave has been designated as FMLA leave may be orally or in writing. If the notice is oral, it shall be confirmed in writing, no laterthan the following payday (unless the

payday is less than one week after the oral notice, in which case the notice must be no later than the subsequent payday). The written notice may be in any form, including a notation on the employee's pay stub.

(c) If the employer requires paid leave to be substituted for unpaid leave, or that paid leave taken under an existing leave plan be counted as FMLA leave, this decision must be made by the employer within two business days of the time the employee gives notice of the need for leave, or, where the employer does not initially have sufficient information to make a determination, when the employer determines that the leave qualifies as FMLA leave if this happens later. The employer's designation must be made before the leave starts, unless the employer does not have sufficient information as to the employee's reason for taking the leave until after the leave commenced. If the employer has the requisite knowledge to make a determination that the paid leave is for an FMLA reason at the time the employee either gives notice of the need for leave or commences leave and fails to designate the leave as FMLA leave (and so notify the employee in accordance with paragraph (b)), the employer may not designate leave as FMLA leave retroactively, and may designate only prospectively as of the date of notification to the employee of the designation. In such circumstances, the employee is subject to the full protections of the Act, but none of the absence preceding the notice to the employee of the designation may be counted against the employee's 12-week FMLA leave entitlement.

(d) If the employer learns that leave is for an FMLA purpose after leave has begun, such as when an employee gives notice of the need for an extension of the paid leave with unpaid FMLA leave, the entire or some portion of the paid leave period may be retroactively counted as FMLA leave, to the extent that the leave period qualified as FMLA leave. For example, an employee is granted two weeks paid vacation leave for a skiing trip. In mid-week of the second week, the employee contacts the employer for an extension of leave as unpaid leave and advises that at the beginning of the second week of paid vacation leave the employee suffered a severe accident requiring hospitalization. The employer may notify the employee that both the extension and the second week of paid vacation leave (from the date of the injury) is designated as FMLA leave. On the other hand, when the employee takes sick leave that turns into a serious health condition (*e.g.*, bronchitis that turns into bronchial pneumonia) and the employee gives notice of the need for an extension of leave, the entire period of the serious health condition may be counted as FMLA leave.

(e) Employers may not designate leave as FMLA leave after the employee has returned to work with two exceptions:

(1) If the employee was absent for an FMLA reason and the employer did not learn the reason for the absence until the employee's return (*e.g.*, where the employee was absent for only a brief period), the employer may, upon

the employee's return to work, promptly (within two business days of the employee's return to work) designate the leave retroactively with appropriate notice to the employee. If leave is taken for an FMLA reason but the employer was not aware of the reason, and the employee desires that the leave be counted as FMLA leave, the employee must notify the employer within two business days of returning to work of the reason for the leave. In the absence of such timely notification by the employee, the employee may not subsequently assert FMLA protections for the absence.

(2) If the employer knows the reason for the leave but has not been able to confirm that the leave qualifies under FMLA, or where the employer has requested medical certification which has not yet been received or the parties are in the process of obtaining a second or third medical opinion, the employer should make a preliminary designation, and so notify the employee, at the time leave begins, or as soon as the reason for the leave becomes known. Upon receipt of the requisite information from the employee or of the medical certification which confirms the leave is for an FMLA reason, the preliminary designation becomes final. If the medical certifications fail to confirm that the reason for the absence was an FMLA reason, the employer must withdraw the designation (with written notice to the employee).

§ 825.209 Is an employee entitled to benefits while using FMLA leave?

(a) During any FMLA leave, an employer must maintain the employee's coverage under any group health plan (as defined in the Internal Revenue Code of 1986 at 26 U.S.C. 5000(b)(1)) on the same conditions as coverage would have been provided if the employee had been continuously employed during the entire leave period. All employers covered by FMLA, including public agencies, are subject to the Act's requirements to maintain health coverage. The definition of "group health plan" is set forth in § 825.800. For purposes of FMLA, the term "group health plan" shall not include an insurance program providing health coverage under which employees purchase individual policies from insurers provided that:

(1) no contributions are made by the employer;

(2) participation in the program is completely voluntary for employees;

(3) the sole functions of the employer with respect to the program are, without endorsing the program, to permit the insurer to publicize the program to employees, to collect premiums through payroll deductions and to remit them to the insurer;

(4) the employer receives no consideration in the form of cash or otherwise in connection with the program, other than reasonable compensation, excluding any profit, for administrative services actually rendered in connection with payroll deduction; and,

(5) the premium charged with respect to such coverage does not increase in the event the employment relationship terminates.

(b) The same group health plan benefits provided to an employee prior to taking FMLA leave must be maintained during the FMLA leave. For example, if family member coverage is provided to an employee, family member coverage must be maintained during the FMLA leave. Similarly, benefit coverage during FMLA leave for medical care, surgical care, hospital care, dental care, eye care, mental health counseling, substance abuse treatment, *etc.*, must be maintained during leave if provided in an employer's group health plan, including a supplement to a group health plan, whether or not provided through a flexible spending account or other component of a cafeteria plan.

(c) If an employer provides a new health plan or benefits or changes health benefits or plans while an employee is on FMLA leave, the employee is entitled to the new or changed plan/benefits to the same extent as if the employee were not on leave. For example, if an employer changes a group health plan so that dental care becomes covered under the plan, an employee on FMLA leave must be given the same opportunity as other employees to receive (or obtain) the dental care coverage. Any other plan changes (*e.g.*, in coverage, premiums, deductibles, *etc.*) which apply to all employees of the workforce would also apply to an employee on FMLA leave.

(d) Notice of any opportunity to change plans or benefits must also be given to an employee on FMLA leave. If the group health plan permits an employee to change from single to family coverage upon the birth of a child or otherwise add new family members, such a change in benefits must be made available while an employee is on FMLA leave. If the employee requests the changed coverage it must be provided by the employer.

(e) An employee may choose not to retain group health plan coverage during FMLA leave. However, when an employee returns from leave, the employee is entitled to be reinstated on the same terms as prior to taking the leave, including family or dependent coverages, without any qualifying period, physical examination, exclusion of pre- existing conditions, *etc. See* § 825.212(c).

(f) Except as required by the Consolidated Omnibus Budget Reconciliation Act of 1986 (COBRA) and for "key" employees (as discussed below), an employer's obligation to maintain health benefits during leave (and to restore the employee to the same or equivalent employment) under FMLA ceases if and when the employment relationship would have terminated if the employee had not taken FMLA leave (*e.g.*, if the employee's position is eliminated as part of a nondiscriminatory reduction in force and the employee would not have been transferred to another position); an employee informs the employer of his or her intent not to return from leave (including before starting the leave if the employer is so informed before the leave starts); or the employee fails to return from leave or continues on leave after exhausting his or her FMLA leave entitlement in the 12 month period.

(g) If a "key employee" (*see* § 825.218) does not return from leave when notified by the employer that substantial or grievous economic injury will result from his or her reinstatement, the employee's entitlement to group health plan benefits continues unless and until the employee advises the employer that the employee does not desire restoration to employment at the end of the leave period, or FMLA leave entitlement is exhausted, or reinstatement is actually denied.

(h) An employee's entitlement to benefits other than group health benefits during a period of FMLA leave (*e.g.*, holiday pay) is to be determined by the employer's established policy for providing such benefits when the employee is on other forms of leave (paid or unpaid, as appropriate).

§ 825.210 How may employees on FMLA leave pay their share of group health benefit premiums?

(a) Group health plan benefits must be maintained on the same basis as coverage would have been provided if the employee had been continuously employed during the FMLA leave period. Therefore, any share of group health plan premiums which had been paid by the employee prior to FMLA leave must continue to be paid by the employee during the FMLA leave period. If premiums are raised or lowered, the employee would be required to pay the new premium rates. Maintenance of health insurance policies which are not a part of the employer's group health plan, as described in § 825.209(a)(1), are the sole responsibility of the employee. The employee and the insurer should make necessary arrangements for payment of premiums during periods of unpaid FMLA leave.

(b) If the FMLA leave is substituted paid leave, the employee's share of premiums must be paid by the method normally used during any paid leave, presumably as a payroll deduction.

(c) If FMLA leave is unpaid, the employer has a number of options for obtaining payment from the employee. The employer may require that payment be made to the employer or to the insurance carrier, but no additional charge may be added to the employee's premium payment for administrative expenses. The employer may require employees to pay their share of premium payments in any of the following ways:

(1) Payment would be due at the same time as it would be made if by payroll deduction;

(2) Payment would be due on the same schedule as payments are made under COBRA;

(3) Payment would be prepaid pursuant to a cafeteria plan at the employee's option;

(4) The employer's existing rules for payment by employees on "leave without pay" would be followed, provided that such rules do not require prepayment (*i.e.*, prior to the commencement of the leave) of the premiums that will become due during a period of unpaid FMLA leave or payment of higher premiums than if the employee had continued to work instead of taking leave; or,

(5) Another system voluntarily agreed to between the employer and the employee, which may include prepayment of premiums (*e.g.*, through increased payroll deductions when the need for the FMLA leave is foreseeable).

(d) The employer must provide the employee with advance written notice of the terms and conditions under which these payments must be made. (*See* § 825.301.)

(e) An employer may not require more of an employee using FMLA leave than the employer requires of other employees on "leave without pay."

(f) An employee who is receiving payments as a result of a workers' compensation injury must make arrangements with the employer for payment of group health plan benefits when simultaneously taking unpaid FMLA leave. *See* paragraph (c) of this section and § 825.207(d)(2).

§ 825.211 What special health benefits maintenance rules apply to multi-employer health plans?

(a) A multi-employer health plan is a plan to which more than one employer is required to contribute, and which is maintained pursuant to one or more collective bargaining agreements between employee organization(s) and the employers.

(b) An employer under a multi-employer plan must continue to make contributions on behalf of an employee using FMLA leave as though the employee had been continuously employed, unless the plan contains an explicit FMLA provision for maintaining coverage such as through pooled contributions by all employers party to the plan.

(c) During the duration of an employee's FMLA leave, coverage by the group health plan, and benefits provided pursuant to the plan, must be maintained at the level of coverage and benefits which were applicable to the employee at the time FMLA leave commenced.

(d) An employee using FMLA leave cannot be required to use "banked" hours or pay a greater premium than the employee would have been required to pay if the employee had been continuously employed.

(e) As provided in § 825.209(f) of this part, group health plan coverage must be maintained for an employee on FMLA leave until:

(1) the employee's FMLA leave entitlement is exhausted;

(2) the employer can show that the employee would have been laid off and the employment relationship terminated; or,

(3) the employee provides unequivocal notice of intent not to return to work.

§ 825.212 What are the consequences of an employee's failure to make timely health plan premium payments?

(a)(1) In the absence of an established employer policy providing a longer grace period, an employer's obligations to maintain health insurance coverage cease under FMLA if an employee's premium payment is more than 30 days late. In order to drop the coverage for an employee whose premium payment is late, the employer must provide written notice to the employee that the payment has not been received. Such notice must be mailed to the employee at least 15 days before coverage is to cease, advising that coverage will be dropped on a specified date at least 15 days after the date of the letter unless the payment has been received by that date. If the employer has established policies regarding other forms of unpaid leave that provide for the employer to cease coverage retroactively to the date the unpaid premium payment was due, the employer may drop the employee from coverage retroactively in accordance with that policy, provided the 15-day notice was given. In the absence of such a policy, coverage for the employee may be terminated at the end of the 30-day grace period, where the required 15 day notice has been provided.

(2) An employer has no obligation regarding the maintenance of a health insurance policy which is not a "group health plan." *See* § 825.209(a).

(3) All other obligations of an employer under FMLA would continue; for example, the employer continues to have an obligation to reinstate an employee upon return from leave.

(b) The employer may recover the employee's share of any premium payments missed by the employee for any FMLA leave period during which the employer maintains health coverage by paying the employee's share after the premium payment is missed.

(c) If coverage lapses because an employee has not made required premium payments, upon the employee's return from FMLA leave the employer must still restore the employee to coverage/benefits equivalent to those the employee would have had if leave had not been taken and the premium payment(s) had not been missed, including family or dependent coverage. *See* § 825.215(d)(1) – (5). In such case, an employee may not be required to meet any qualification requirements imposed by the plan, including any new preexisting condition waiting period, to wait for an open season, or to pass a medical examination to obtain reinstatement of coverage.

§ 825.213 May an employer recover costs it incurred for maintaining "group health plan" or other non-health benefits coverage during FMLA leave?

(a) In addition to the circumstances discussed in § 825.212(b), an employer may recover its share of health plan premiums during a period of unpaid FMLA leave from an employee if the employee fails to return to work after the employee's FMLA leave entitlement has been exhausted or expires, unless the reason the employee does not return is due to:

(1) The continuation, recurrence, or onset of a serious health condition of the employee or the employee's family member which would otherwise entitle the employee to leave under FMLA; or

(2) Other circumstances beyond the employee's control. Examples of "other circumstances beyond the employee's control" are necessarily broad. They include such situations as where a parent chooses to stay home with a newborn child who has a serious health condition; an employee's spouse is unexpectedly transferred to a job location more than 75 miles from the employee's worksite; a relative or individual other than an immediate family member has a serious health condition and the employee is needed to provide care; the employee is laid off while on leave; or, the employee is a "key employee" who decides not to return to work upon being notified of the employer's intention to deny restoration because of substantial and grievous economic injury to the employer's operations and is not reinstated by the employer. Other circumstances beyond the employee's control would not include a situation where an employee desires to remain with a parent in a distant city even though the parent no longer requires the employee's care, or a parent chooses not to return to work to stay home with a well, newborn child.

(3) When an employee fails to return to work because of the continuation, recurrence, or onset of a serious health condition, thereby precluding the employer from recovering its (share of) health benefit premium payments made on the employee's behalf during a period of unpaid FMLA leave, the employer may require medical certification of the employee's or the family member's serious health condition. Such certification is not required unless requested by the employer. The employee is required to provide medical certification in a timely manner which, for purposes of this section, is within 30 days from the date of the employer's request. For purposes of medical certification, the employee may use the optional DOL form developed for this purpose (*see* § 825.306(a) and Appendix B of this

part [Appendix E of this volume]). If the employer requests medical certification and the employee does not provide such certification in a timely manner (within 30 days), or the reason for not returning to work does not meet the test of other circumstances beyond the employee's control, the employer may recover 100% of the health benefit premiums it paid during the period of unpaid FMLA leave.

(b) Under some circumstances an employer may elect to maintain other benefits, *e.g.*, life insurance, disability insurance, *etc.*, by paying the employee's (share of) premiums during periods of unpaid FMLA leave. For example, to ensure the employer can meet its responsibilities to provide equivalent benefits to the employee upon return from unpaid FMLA leave, it may be necessary that premiums be paid continuously to avoid a lapse of coverage. If the employer elects to maintain such benefits during the leave, at the conclusion of leave, the employer is entitled to recover only the costs incurred for paying the employee's share of any premiums whether or not the employee returns to work.

(c) An employee who returns to work for at least 30 calendar days is considered to have "returned" to work. An employee who transfers directly from taking FMLA leave to retirement, or who retires during the first 30 days after the employee returns to work, is deemed to have returned to work.

(d) When an employee elects or an employer requires paid leave to be substituted for FMLA leave, the employer may not recover its (share of) health insurance or other non-health benefit premiums for any period of FMLA leave covered by paid leave. Because paid leave provided under a plan covering temporary disabilities (including workers' compensation) is not unpaid, recovery of health insurance premiums does not apply to such paid leave.

(e) The amount that self-insured employers may recover is limited to only the employer's share of allowable "premiums" as would be calculated under COBRA, excluding the 2 percent fee for administrative costs.

(f) When an employee fails to return to work, any health and non-health benefit premiums which this section of the regulations permits an employer to recover are a debt owed by the non-returning employee to the employer. The existence of this debt caused by the employee's failure to return to work does not alter the employer's responsibilities for health benefit coverage and, under a self-insurance plan, payment of claims incurred during the period of FMLA leave. To the extent recovery is allowed, the employer may recover the costs through deduction from any sums due to the employee (*e.g.*, unpaid wages, vacation pay, profit sharing, *etc.*), provided such deductions do not otherwise violate applicable Federal or State wage payment or other laws. Alternatively, the employer may initiate legal action against the employee to recover such costs.

§ 825.214 What are an employee's rights on returning to work from FMLA leave?

(a) On return from FMLA leave, an employee is entitled to be returned to the same position the employee held when leave commenced, or to an equivalent position with equivalent benefits, pay, and other terms and conditions of employment. An employee is entitled to such reinstatement even if the employee has been replaced or his or her position has been restructured to accommodate the employee's absence. *See also* § 825.106(e) for the obligations of joint employers.

(b) If the employee is unable to perform an essential function of the position because of a physical or mental condition, including the continuation of a serious health condition, the employee has no right to restoration to another position under the FMLA. However, the employer's obligations may be governed by the Americans with Disabilities Act (ADA). *See* § 825.702.

§ 825.215 What is an equivalent position?

(a) An equivalent position is one that is virtually identical to the employee's former position in terms of pay, benefits and working conditions, including privileges, perquisites and status. It must involve the same or substantially similar duties and responsibilities, which must entail substantially equivalent skill, effort, responsibility, and authority.

(b) If an employee is no longer qualified for the position because of the employee's inability to attend a necessary course, renew a license, fly a minimum number of hours, *etc.*, as a result of the leave, the employee shall be given a reasonable opportunity to fulfill those conditions upon return to work.

(c) *Equivalent Pay.*

(1) An employee is entitled to any unconditional pay increases which may have occurred during the FMLA leave period, such as cost of living increases. Pay increases conditioned upon seniority, length of service, or work performed would not have to be granted unless it is the employer's policy or practice to do so with respect to other employees on "leave without pay." In such case, any pay increase would be granted based on the employee's seniority, length of service, work performed, *etc.*, excluding the period of unpaid FMLA leave. An employee is entitled to be restored to a position with the same or equivalent pay premiums, such as a shift differential. If an employee departed from a position averaging ten hours of overtime (and corresponding overtime pay) each week, an employee is ordinarily entitled to such a position on return from FMLA leave.

(2) Many employers pay bonuses in different forms to employees for job-related performance such as for perfect attendance, safety (absence of

injuries or accidents on the job) and exceeding production goals. Bonuses for perfect attendance and safety do not require performance by the employee but rather contemplate the absence of occurrences. To the extent an employee who takes FMLA leave had met all the requirements for either or both of these bonuses before FMLA leave began, the employee is entitled to continue this entitlement upon return from FMLA leave, that is, the employee may not be disqualified for the bonus(es) for the taking of FMLA leave. *See* § 825.220 (b) and (c). A monthly production bonus, on the other hand does require performance by the employee. If the employee is on FMLA leave during any part of the period for which the bonus is computed, the employee is entitled to the same consideration for the bonus as other employees on paid or unpaid leave (as appropriate). *See* paragraph (d)(2) of this section.

(d) *Equivalent Benefits.* "Benefits" include all benefits provided or made available to employees by an employer, including group life insurance, health insurance, disability insurance, sick leave, annual leave, educational benefits, and pensions, regardless of whether such benefits are provided by a practice or written policy of an employer through an employee benefit plan as defined in Section 3(3) of the Employee Retirement Income Security Act of 1974, 29 U.S.C. 1002(3).

(1) At the end of an employee's FMLA leave, benefits must be resumed in the same manner and at the same levels as provided when the leave began, and subject to any changes in benefit levels that may have taken place during the period of FMLA leave affecting the entire workforce, unless otherwise elected by the employee. Upon return from FMLA leave, an employee cannot be required to requalify for any benefits the employee enjoyed before FMLA leave began (including family or dependent coverages). For example, if an employee was covered by a life insurance policy before taking leave but is not covered or coverage lapses during the period of unpaid FMLA leave, the employee cannot be required to meet any qualifications, such as taking a physical examination, in order to requalify for life insurance upon return from leave. Accordingly, some employers may find it necessary to modify life insurance and other benefits programs in order to restore employees to equivalent benefits upon return from FMLA leave, make arrangements for continued payment of costs to maintain such benefits during unpaid FMLA leave, or pay these costs subject to recovery from the employee on return from leave. *See* § 825.213(b).

(2) An employee may, but is not entitled to, accrue any additional benefits or seniority during unpaid FMLA leave. Benefits accrued at the time leave began, however, (*e.g.*, paid vacation, sick or personal leave to the extent not substituted for FMLA leave) must be available to an employee upon return from leave.

(3) If, while on unpaid FMLA leave, an employee desires to continue life insurance, disability insurance, or other types of benefits for which he or she typically pays, the employer is required to follow established policies or practices for continuing such benefits for other instances of leave without pay. If the employer has no established policy, the employee and the employer are encouraged to agree upon arrangements before FMLA leave begins.

(4) With respect to pension and other retirement plans, any period of unpaid FMLA leave shall not be treated as or counted toward a break in service for purposes of vesting and eligibility to participate. Also, if the plan requires an employee to be employed on a specific date in order to be credited with a year of service for vesting, contributions or participation purposes, an employee on unpaid FMLA leave on that date shall be deemed to have been employed on that date. However, unpaid FMLA leave periods need not be treated as credited service for purposes of benefit accrual, vesting and eligibility to participate.

(5) Employees on unpaid FMLA leave are to be treated as if they continued to work for purposes of changes to benefit plans. They are entitled to changes in benefits plans, except those which may be dependent upon seniority or accrual during the leave period, immediately upon return from leave or to the same extent they would have qualified if no leave had been taken. For example if the benefit plan is predicated on a pre-established number of hours worked each year and the employee does not have sufficient hours as a result of taking unpaid FMLA leave, the benefit is lost. (In this regard, § 825.209 addresses health benefits.)

(e) *Equivalent Terms and Conditions of Employment.* An equivalent position must have substantially similar duties, conditions, responsibilities, privileges and status as the employee's original position.

(1) The employee must be reinstated to the same or a geographically proximate worksite (*i.e.*, one that does not involve a significant increase in commuting time or distance) from where the employee had previously been employed. If the employee's original worksite has been closed, the employee is entitled to the same rights as if the employee had not been on leave when the worksite closed. For example, if an employer transfers all employees from a closed worksite to a new worksite in a different city, the employee on leave is also entitled to transfer under the same conditions as if he or she had continued to be employed.

(2) The employee is ordinarily entitled to return to the same shift or the same or an equivalent work schedule.

(3) The employee must have the same or an equivalent opportunity for bonuses, profit-sharing, and other similar discretionary and non-discretionary payments.

(4) FMLA does not prohibit an employer from accommodating an employee's request to be restored to a different shift, schedule, or position

which better suits the employee's personal needs on return from leave, or to offer a promotion to a better position. However, an employee cannot be induced by the employer to accept a different position against the employee's wishes.

(f) The requirement that an employee be restored to the same or equivalent job with the same or equivalent pay, benefits, and terms and conditions of employment does not extend to *de minimis* or intangible, unmeasurable aspects of the job. However, restoration to a job slated for lay-off when the employee's original position is not would not meet the requirements of an equivalent position.

§ 825.216 Are there any limitations on an employer's obligation to reinstate an employee?

(a) An employee has no greater right to reinstatement or to other benefits and conditions of employment than if the employee had been continuously employed during the FMLA leave period. An employer must be able to show that an employee would not otherwise have been employed at the time reinstatement is requested in order to deny restoration to employment. For example:

(1) If an employee is laid off during the course of taking FMLA leave and employment is terminated, the employer's responsibility to continue FMLA leave, maintain group health plan benefits and restore the employee cease at the time the employee is laid off, provided the employer has no continuing obligations under a collective bargaining agreement or otherwise. An employer would have the burden of proving that an employee would have been laid off during the FMLA leave period and, therefore, would not be entitled to restoration.

(2) If a shift has been eliminated, or overtime has been decreased, an employee would not be entitled to return to work that shift or the original overtime hours upon restoration. However, if a position on, for example, a night shift has been filled by another employee, the employee is entitled to return to the same shift on which employed before taking FMLA leave.

(b) If an employee was hired for a specific term or only to perform work on a discrete project, the employer has no obligation to restore the employee if the employment term or project is over and the employer would not otherwise have continued to employ the employee. On the other hand, if an employee was hired to perform work on a contract, and after that contract period the contract was awarded to another contractor, the successor contractor may be required to restore the employee if it is a successor employer. *See* § 825.107.

(c) In addition to the circumstances explained above, an employer may deny job restoration to salaried eligible employees ("key employees," as defined in paragraph (c) of § 825.217) if such denial is necessary to prevent substantial and grievous economic injury to the operations of the employer; or may delay restoration to an employee who fails to provide a fitness for duty certificate to return to work under the conditions described in § 825.310.

(d) If the employee has been on a workers' compensation absence during which FMLA leave has been taken concurrently, and after 12 weeks of FMLA leave the employee is unable to return to work, the employee no longer has the protections of FMLA and must look to the workers' compensation statute or ADA for any relief or protections.

§ 825.217 What is a "key employee"?

(a) A "key employee" is a salaried FMLA-eligible employee who is among the highest paid 10 percent of all the employees employed by the employer within 75 miles of the employee's worksite.

(b) The term "salaried" means "paid on a salary basis," as defined in 29 CFR 541.118. This is the Department of Labor regulation defining employees who may qualify as exempt from the minimum wage and overtime requirements of the FLSA as executive, administrative, and professional employees.

(c) A "key employee" must be "among the highest paid 10 percent" of all the employees — both salaried and non-salaried, eligible and ineligible — who are employed by the employer within 75 miles of the worksite.

(1) In determining which employees are among the highest paid 10 percent, year-to-date earnings are divided by weeks worked by the employee (including weeks in which paid leave was taken). Earnings include wages, premium pay, incentive pay, and non-discretionary and discretionary bonuses. Earnings do not include incentives whose value is determined at some future date, *e.g.*, stock options, or benefits or perquisites.

(2) The determination of whether a salaried employee is among the highest paid 10 percent shall be made at the time the employee gives notice of the need for leave. No more than 10 percent of the employer's employees within 75 miles of the worksite may be "key employees."

§ 825.218 What does "substantial and grievous economic injury" mean?

(a) In order to deny restoration to a key employee, an employer must determine that the restoration of the employee to employment will cause "substantial and grievous economic injury" to the operations of the employer, not whether the absence of the employee will cause such substantial and grievous injury.

(b) An employer may take into account its ability to replace on a temporary basis (or temporarily do without) the employee on FMLA leave. If permanent replacement is unavoidable, the cost of then reinstating the employee can be considered in evaluating whether substantial and grievous economic injury will occur from restoration; in other words, the effect on the operations of the company of reinstating the employee in an equivalent position.

(c) A precise test cannot be set for the level of hardship or injury to the employer which must be sustained. If the reinstatement of a "key employee" threatens the economic viability of the firm, that would constitute "substantial and grievous economic injury." A lesser injury which causes substantial, long-term economic injury would also be sufficient. Minor inconveniences and costs that the employer would experience in the normal course of doing business would certainly not constitute "substantial and grievous economic injury."

(d) FMLA's "substantial and grievous economic injury" standard is different from and more stringent than the "undue hardship" test under the ADA (*see also* § 825.702).

§ 825.219 What are the rights of a key employee?

(a) An employer who believes that reinstatement may be denied to a key employee, must give written notice to the employee at the time the employee gives notice of the need for FMLA leave (or when FMLA leave commences, if earlier) that he or she qualifies as a key employee. At the same time, the employer must also fully inform the employee of the potential consequences with respect to reinstatement and maintenance of health benefits if the employer should determine that substantial and grievous economic injury to the employer's operations will result if the employee is reinstated from FMLA leave. If such notice cannot be given immediately because of the need to determine whether the employee is a key employee, it shall be given as soon as practicable after being notified of a need for leave (or the commencement of leave, if earlier). It is expected that in most circumstances there will be no desire that an employee be denied restoration after FMLA leave and, therefore, there would be no need to provide such notice. However, an employer who fails to provide such timely notice will lose its right to deny restoration even if substantial and grievous economic injury will result from reinstatement.

(b) As soon as an employer makes a good faith determination, based on the facts available, that substantial and grievous economic injury to its operations will result if a key employee who has given notice of the need for FMLA leave or is using FMLA leave is reinstated, the employer shall notify the employee in writing of its determination, that it cannot deny FMLA leave, and that it intends to deny restoration to employment on completion of the FMLA leave. It is anticipated that an employer will ordinarily be able to give such notice prior to the employee starting leave. The employer must serve this notice either in person or by certified mail. This notice must explain the basis for the employer's finding that substantial and grievous economic injury will result, and, if leave has commenced, must provide the employee a reasonable time in which to return to work, taking into account the circumstances, such as the length of the leave and the urgency of the need for the employee to return.

(c) If an employee on leave does not return to work in response to the employer's notification of intent to deny restoration, the employee continues to be entitled to maintenance of health benefits and the employer may not recover its cost of health benefit premiums. A key employee's rights under FMLA continue unless and until the employee either gives notice that he or she no longer wishes to return to work, or the employer actually denies reinstatement at the conclusion of the leave period.

(d) After notice to an employee has been given that substantial and grievous economic injury will result if the employee is reinstated to employment, an employee is still entitled to request reinstatement at the end of the leave period even if the employee did not return to work in response to the employer's notice. The employer must then again determine whether there will be substantial and grievous economic injury from reinstatement, based on the facts at that time. If it is determined that substantial and grievous economic injury will result, the employer shall notify the employee in writing (in person or by certified mail) of the denial of restoration.

§ 825.220 How are employees protected who request leave or otherwise assert FMLA rights?

(a) The FMLA prohibits interference with an employee's rights under the law, and with legal proceedings or inquiries relating to an employee's rights. More specifically, the law contains the following employee protections:

(1) An employer is prohibited from interfering with, restraining, or denying the exercise of (or attempts to exercise) any rights provided by the Act.

(2) An employer is prohibited from discharging or in any other way discriminating against any person (whether or not an employee) for opposing or complaining about any unlawful practice under the Act.

(3) All persons (whether or not employers) are prohibited from discharging or in any other way discriminating against any person (whether or not an employee) because that person has—

(i) Filed any charge, or has instituted (or caused to be instituted) any proceeding under or related to this Act;

(ii) Given, or is about to give, any information in connection with an inquiry or proceeding relating to a right under this Act;

(iii) Testified, or is about to testify, in any inquiry or proceeding relating to a right under this Act.

(b) Any violations of the Act or of these regulations constitute interfering with, restraining, or denying the exercise of rights provided by the Act. "Interfering with" the exercise of an employee's rights would include, for example, not only refusing to authorize FMLA leave, but discouraging an employee from using such leave. It would also include manipulation by a covered employer to avoid responsibilities under FMLA, for example:

(1) transferring employees from one worksite to another for the purpose of reducing worksites, or to keep worksites, below the 50-employee threshold for employee eligibility under the Act;

(2) changing the essential functions of the job in order to preclude the taking of leave;

(3) reducing hours available to work in order to avoid employee eligibility.

(c) An employer is prohibited from discriminating against employees or prospective employees who have used FMLA leave. For example, if an employee on leave without pay would otherwise be entitled to full benefits (other than health benefits), the same benefits would be required to be provided to an employee on unpaid FMLA leave. By the same token, employers cannot use the taking of FMLA leave as a negative factor in employment actions, such as hiring, promotions or disciplinary actions; nor can FMLA leave be counted under "no fault" attendance policies.

(d) Employees cannot waive, nor may employers induce employees to waive, their rights under FMLA. For example, employees (or their collective bargaining representatives) cannot "trade off" the right to take FMLA leave against some other benefit offered by the employer. This does not prevent an employee's voluntary and uncoerced acceptance (not as a condition of employment) of a "light duty" assignment while recovering from a serious health condition (*see* § 825.702(d)). In such a circumstance the employee's right to restoration to the same or an equivalent position is available until 12 weeks have passed within the 12-month period, including all FMLA leave taken and the period of "light duty."

(e) Individuals, and not merely employees, are protected from retaliation for opposing (*e.g.*, file a complaint about) any practice which is unlawful under the Act. They are similarly protected if they oppose any practice which they reasonably believe to be a violation of the Act or regulations.

SUBPART C
How do employees learn of their FMLA rights and obligations, and what can an employer require of an employee?

§ 825.300 What posting requirements does the Act place on employers?

(a) Every employer covered by the FMLA is required to post and keep posted on its premises, in conspicuous places where employees are employed, whether or not it has any "eligible" employees, a notice explaining the Act's provisions and providing information concerning the procedures for filing complaints of violations of the Act with the Wage and Hour Division. The notice must be posted prominently where it can be readily seen by employees and applicants for employment. Employers may duplicate the text of the notice contained in Appendix C of this part [Appendix F of this volume], or copies of the required notice may be obtained from local offices of the Wage and Hour Division. The poster and the text must be large enough to be easily read and contain fully legible text.

(b) An employer that willfully violates the posting requirement may be assessed a civil money penalty by the Wage and Hour Division not to exceed $100 for each separate offense. Furthermore, an employer that fails to post the required notice cannot take any adverse action against an employee, including denying FMLA leave, for failing to furnish the employer with advance notice of a need to take FMLA leave.

(c) Where an employer's workforce is comprised of a significant portion of workers who are not literate in English, the employer shall be responsible for providing the notice in a language in which the employees are literate.

§ 825.301 What other notices to employees are required of employers under the FMLA?

(a)(1) If an FMLA-covered employer has any eligible employees and has any written guidance to employees concerning employee benefits or leave rights, such as in an employee handbook, information concerning FMLA entitlements and employee obligations under the FMLA must be included in the handbook or other document. For example, if an employer provides an employee handbook to all employees that describes the employer's policies regarding leave, wages, attendance, and similar matters, the handbook must incorporate information on FMLA rights and responsibilities and the employer's policies regarding the FMLA. Informational publications describing the Act's provisions are available from local offices of the Wage and Hour Division and may be incorporated in such employer handbooks or written policies.

(2) If such an employer does not have written policies, manuals, or handbooks describing employee benefits and leave provisions, the employer shall provide written guidance to an employee concerning all the employee's rights and obligations under the FMLA. This notice shall be provided to employees each time notice is given pursuant to paragraph (b), and in accordance with the provisions of that paragraph. Employers may duplicate and provide the employee a copy of the FMLA Fact Sheet available from the nearest office of the Wage and Hour Division to provide such guidance.

(b)(1) The employer shall also provide the employee with written notice detailing the specific expectations and obligations of the employee and explaining any consequences of a failure to meet these obligations. The written notice must be provided to the employee in a language in which the employee is literate (*see* § 825.300(c)). Such specific notice must include, as appropriate:

(i) that the leave will be counted against the employee's annual FMLA leave entitlement (*see* § 825.208);

(ii) any requirements for the employee to furnish medical certification of a serious health condition and the consequences of failing to do so (*see* § 825.305);

(iii) the employee's right to substitute paid leave and whether the employer will require the substitution of paid leave, and the conditions related to any substitution;

(iv) any requirement for the employee to make any premium payments to maintain health benefits and the arrangements for making such payments (*see* § 825.210), and the possible consequences of failure to make such payments on a timely basis (*i.e.*, the circumstances under which coverage may lapse);

(v) any requirement for the employee to present a fitness for-duty certificate to be restored to employment (*see* § 825.310);

(vi) the employee's status as a "key employee" and the potential consequence that restoration may be denied following FMLA leave, explaining the conditions required for such denial (*see* § 825.218);

(vii) the employee's right to restoration to the same or an equivalent job upon return from leave (*see* § 825.214 and 825.604); and,

(viii) the employee's potential liability for payment of health insurance premiums paid by the employer during the employee's unpaid FMLA leave if the employee fails to return to work after taking FMLA leave (*see* § 825.213).

(2) The specific notice may include other information-*e.g.*, whether the employer will require periodic reports of the employee's status and intent to return to work, but is not required to do so. A prototype notice is contained in Appendix D of this part [Appendix G of this volume], or may be obtained from local offices of the Department of Labor's Wage and Hour Division, which employers may adapt for their use to meet these specific notice requirements.

(c) Except as provided in this subparagraph, the written notice required by paragraph (b) (and by subparagraph (a)(2) where applicable) must be provided to the employee no less often than the first time in each six-month period that an employee gives notice of the need for FMLA leave (if FMLA leave is taken during the six-month period). The notice shall be given within a reasonable time after notice of the need for leave is given by the employee-within one or two business days if feasible. If leave has already begun, the notice should be mailed to the employee's address of record.

(1) If the specific information provided by the notice changes with respect to a subsequent period of FMLA leave during the six-month period, the employer shall, within one or two business days of receipt of the employee's notice of need for leave, provide written notice referencing the prior notice and setting forth any of the information in subparagraph (b) which has changed. For example, if the initial leave period were paid leave and the subsequent leave period would be unpaid leave, the employer may need to give notice of the arrangements for making premium payments.

(2)(i) Except as provided in subparagraph (ii), if the employer is requiring medical certification or a "fitness-for-duty" report, written notice of the requirement shall be given with respect to each employee notice of a need for leave.

(ii) Subsequent written notification shall not be required if the initial notice in the six-months period and the employer handbook or other written documents (if any) describing the employer's leave policies, clearly provided that certification or a "fitness-for-duty" report would be required (e.g., by stating that certification would be required in all cases, by stating that certification would be required in all cases in which leave of more than a specified number of days is taken, or by stating that a "fitness-for-duty" report would be required in all cases for back injuries for employees in a certain occupation). Where subsequent written notice is not required, at least oral notice shall be provided. (See § 825.305(a).)

(d) Employers are also expected to responsively answer questions from employees concerning their rights and responsibilities under the FMLA.

(e) Employers furnishing FMLA-required notices to sensory impaired individuals must also comply with all applicable requirements under Federal or State law.

(f) If an employer fails to provide notice in accordance with the provisions of this section, the employer may not take action against an employee for failure to comply with any provision required to be set forth in the notice.

§ 825.302 What notice does an employee have to give an employer when the need for FMLA leave is foreseeable?

(a) An employee must provide the employer at least 30 days advance notice before FMLA leave is to begin if the need for the leave is foreseeable based on an expected birth, placement for adoption or foster care, or planned medical treatment for a serious health condition of the employee or of a family member. If 30 days notice is not practicable, such as because of a lack of knowledge of approximately when leave will be required to begin, a change in circumstances, or a medical emergency, notice must be given as soon as practicable. For example, an employee's health condition may require leave to commence earlier than anticipated before the birth of a child. Similarly, little opportunity for notice may be given before placement for adoption. Whether the leave is to be continuous or is to be taken intermittently or on a reduced schedule basis, notice need only be given one time, but the employee shall advise the employer as soon as practicable if dates of scheduled leave change or are extended, or were initially unknown.

(b) "As soon as practicable" means as soon as both possible and practical, taking into account all of the facts and circumstances in the individual case. For foreseeable leave where it is not possible to give as much as 30 days notice, "as soon as practicable" ordinarily would mean at least verbal notification to the employer within one or two business days of when the need for leave becomes known to the employee.

(c) An employee shall provide at least verbal notice sufficient to make the employer aware that the employee needs FMLA-qualifying leave, and the anticipated timing and duration of the leave. The employee need not expressly assert rights under the FMLA or even mention the FMLA, but may only state that leave is needed for an expected birth or adoption, for example. The employer should inquire further of the employee if it is necessary to have more information about whether FMLA leave is being sought by the employee, and obtain the necessary details of the leave to be taken. In the case of medical conditions, the employer may find it necessary to inquire further to determine if the leave is because of a serious health condition and may request medical certification to support the need for such leave (*see* § 825.305).

(d) An employer may also require an employee to comply with the employer's usual and customary notice and procedural requirements for requesting leave. For example, an employer may require that written notice set forth the reasons for the requested leave, the anticipated duration of the leave, and the anticipated start of the leave. However, failure to follow such internal employer procedures will not permit an employer to disallow or delay an employee's taking FMLA leave if the employee gives timely verbal or other notice.

(e) When planning medical treatment, the employee must consult with the employer and make a reasonable effort to schedule the leave so as not to disrupt unduly the employer's operations, subject to the approval of the health care provider. Employees are ordinarily expected to consult with their employers prior to the scheduling of treatment in order to work out a treatment schedule which best suits the needs of both the employer and the employee. If an employee who provides notice of the need to take FMLA leave on an intermittent basis for planned medical treatment neglects to consult with the employer to make a reasonable attempt to arrange the schedule of treatments so as not to unduly disrupt the employer's operations, the employer may initiate discussions with the employee and require the employee to attempt to make such arrangements, subject to the approval of the health care provider.

(f) In the case of intermittent leave or leave on a reduced leave schedule which is medically necessary, an employee shall advise the employer, upon request, of the reasons why the intermittent/reduced leave schedule is necessary and of the schedule for treatment, if applicable. The employee and employer shall attempt to work out a schedule which meets the employee's needs without unduly disrupting the employer's operations, subject to the approval of the health care provider.

(g) An employer may waive employees' FMLA notice requirements. In addition, an employer may not require compliance with stricter FMLA notice requirements where the provisions of a collective bargaining agreement, State law, or applicable leave plan allow less advance notice to the employer. For example, if an employee (or employer) elects to substitute paid vacation leave for unpaid FMLA leave (*see* § 825.207), and the employer's paid vacation leave plan imposes no prior notification requirements for taking such vacation leave, no advance notice may be required for the FMLA leave taken in these circumstances. On the other hand, FMLA notice requirements would apply to a period of unpaid FMLA leave, unless the employer imposes lesser notice requirements on employees taking leave without pay.

§ 825.303 What are the requirements for an employee to furnish notice to an employer where the need for FMLA leave is not foreseeable?

(a) When the approximate timing of the need for leave is not foreseeable, an employee should give notice to the employer of the need for FMLA leave as soon as practicable under the facts and circumstances of the particular case. It is expected that an employee will give notice to the employer within no more than one or two working days of learning of the need for leave, except in extraordinary circumstances where such notice is not feasible. In the case of a medical emergency requiring leave because of an employee's own serious health condition or to care for a family member with a serious health condition, written advance notice pursuant to an employer's internal rules and procedures may not be required when FMLA leave is involved.

(b) The employee should provide notice to the employer either in person or by telephone, telegraph, facsimile ("fax") machine or other electronic means. Notice may be given by the employee's spokesperson (*e.g.*, spouse, adult family member or other responsible party) if the employee is unable to do so personally. The employee need not expressly assert rights under the FMLA or even mention the FMLA, but may only state that leave is needed. The employer will be expected to obtain any additional required information through informal means. The employee or spokesperson will be expected to provide more information when it can readily be accomplished as a practical matter, taking into consideration the exigencies of the situation.

§ 825.304 What recourse do employers have if employees fail to provide the required notice?

(a) An employer may waive employees' FMLA notice obligations or the employer's own internal rules on leave notice requirements.

(b) If an employee fails to give 30 days notice for foreseeable leave with no reasonable excuse for the delay, the employer may delay the taking of FMLA leave until at least 30 days after the date the employee provides notice to the employer of the need for FMLA leave.

(c) In all cases, in order for the onset of an employee's FMLA leave to be delayed due to lack of required notice, it must be clear that the employee had actual notice of the FMLA notice requirements. This condition would be satisfied by the employer's proper posting of the required notice at the worksite where the employee is employed. Furthermore, the need for leave and the approximate date leave would be taken must have been clearly foreseeable to the employee 30 days in advance of the leave. For example, knowledge that an employee would receive a telephone call about the availability of a child for adoption at some unknown point in the future would not be sufficient.

§ 825.305 When must an employee provide medical certification to support FMLA leave?

(a) An employer may require that an employee's leave to care for the employee's seriously-ill spouse, son, daughter, or parent, or due to the employee's own serious health condition that makes the employee unable to perform one or more of the essential functions of the employee's position, be supported by a certification issued by the health care provider of the employee or the employee's ill family member. An employer must give notice of a requirement for medical certification each time a certification is required; such notice must be written notice whenever required by § 825.301. An employer's oral request to an employee to furnish any subsequent medical certification is sufficient.

(b) When the leave is foreseeable and at least 30 days notice has been provided, the employee should provide the medical certification before the leave begins. When this is not possible, the employee must provide the requested certification to the employer within the time frame requested by the employer (which must allow at least 15 calendar days after the employer's request), unless it is not practicable under the particular circumstances to do so despite the employee's diligent, good faith efforts.

(c) In most cases, the employer should request that an employee furnish certification from a health care provider at the time the employee gives notice of the need for leave or within two business days thereafter, or, in the case of unforeseen leave, within two business days after the leave commences. The employer may request certification at some later date if the employer later has reason to question the appropriateness of the leave or its duration.

(d) At the time the employer requests certification, the employer must also advise an employee of the anticipated consequences of an employee's failure to provide adequate certification. The employer shall advise an employee whenever the employer finds a certification incomplete, and provide the employee a reasonable opportunity to cure any such deficiency.

(e) If the employer's sick or medical leave plan imposes medical certification requirements that are less stringent than the certification requirements of these regulations, and the employee or employer elects to substitute paid sick, vacation, personal or family leave for unpaid FMLA leave where authorized (*see* § 825.207), only the employer's less stringent sick leave certification requirements may be imposed.

§ 825.306 How much information may be required in medical certifications of a serious health condition?

(a) DOL has developed an optional form (Form WH-380, as revised) for employees' (or their family members') use in obtaining medical certification, including second and third opinions, from health care providers that meets FMLA's certification requirements. (*See* Appendix B to these regulations.) This optional form reflects certification requirements so as to permit the health care provider to furnish appropriate medical information within his or her knowledge.

(b) Form WH-380, as revised, or another form containing the same basic information, may be used by the employer; however, no additional information may be required. In all instances the information on the form must relate only to the serious health condition for which the current need for leave exists. The form identifies the health care provider and type of medical practice (including pertinent specialization, if any), makes maximum use of checklist entries for ease in completing the form, and contains required entries for:

(1) A certification as to which part of the definition of "serious health condition" (*see* § 825.114), if any, applies to the patient's condition, and the medical facts which support the certification, including a brief statement as to how the medical facts meet the criteria of the definition.

(2)(i) The approximate date the serious health condition commenced, and its probable duration, including the probable duration of the patient's present incapacity (defined to mean inability to work, attend school or perform other regular daily activities due to the serious health condition, treatment therefor, or recovery therefrom) if different.

(ii) Whether it will be necessary for the employee to take leave intermittently or to work on a reduced leave schedule basis (*i.e.*, part-time) as a result of the serious health condition (*see* § 825.117 and § 825.203), and if so, the probable duration of such schedule.

(iii) If the condition is pregnancy or a chronic condition within the meaning of § 825.114(a)(2)(iii), whether the patient is presently incapacitated and the likely duration and frequency of episodes of incapacity.

(3)(i)(A) If additional treatments will be required for the condition, an estimate of the probable number of such treatments.

(B) If the patient's incapacity will be intermittent, or will require a reduced leave schedule, an estimate of the probable number and interval between such treatments, actual or estimated dates of treatment if known, and period required for recovery if any.

(ii) If any of the treatments referred to in subparagraph (i) will be provided by another provider of health services (*e.g.*, physical therapist), the nature of the treatments.

(iii) If a regimen of continuing treatment by the patient is required under the supervision of the health care provider, a general description of the regimen (*see* § 825.114(b)).

(4) If medical leave is required for the employee's absence from work because of the employee's own condition (including absences due to pregnancy or a chronic condition), whether the employee:

(i) Is unable to perform work of any kind;

(ii) Is unable to perform any one or more of the essential functions of the employee's position, including a statement of the essential functions the employee is unable to perform (*see* § 825.115), based on either information provided on a statement from the employer of the essential functions of the position or, if not provided, discussion with the employee about the employee's job functions; or

(iii) Must be absent from work for treatment.

(5)(i) If leave is required to care for a family member of the employee with a serious health condition, whether the patient requires assistance for basic medical or personal needs or safety, or for transportation; or if not, whether the employee's presence to provide psychological comfort would be beneficial to the patient or assist in the patient's recovery. The employee is required to indicate on the form the care he or she will provide and an estimate of the time period.

(ii) If the employee's family member will need care only intermittently or on a reduced leave schedule basis (*i.e.*, part time), the probable duration of the need.

(c) If the employer's sick or medical leave plan requires less information to be furnished in medical certifications than the certification requirements of these regulations, and the employee or employer elects to substitute paid sick, vacation, personal or family leave for unpaid FMLA leave where authorized (*see* § 825.207), only the employer's lesser sick leave certification requirements may be imposed.

§ 825.307 What may an employer do if it questions the adequacy of a medical certification?

(a) If an employee submits a complete certification signed by the health care provider, the employer may not request additional information from the employee's health care provider. However, a health care provider representing the employer may contact the employee's health care provider, with the employee's permission, for purposes of clarification and authenticity of the medical certification.

(1) If an employee is on FMLA leave running concurrently with a workers' compensation absence, and the provisions of the workers' compensation statute permit the employer or the employer's representative to have direct contact with the employee's workers' compensation health care provider, the employer may follow the workers' compensation provisions.

(2) An employer who has reason to doubt the validity of a medical certification may require the employee to obtain a second opinion at the employer's expense. Pending receipt of the second (or third) medical opinion, the employee is provisionally entitled to the benefits of the Act, including maintenance of group health benefits. If the certifications do not ultimately establish the employee's entitlement to FMLA leave, the leave shall not be designated as FMLA leave and may be treated as paid or unpaid leave under the employer's established leave policies. The employer is permitted to designate the health care provider to furnish the second opinion, but the selected health care provider may not be employed on a regular basis by the employer. *See also* paragraphs (e) and (f) of this section.

(b) The employer may not regularly contract with or otherwise regularly utilize the services of the health care provider furnishing the second opinion unless the employer is located in an area where access to health care is extremely limited (*e.g.*, a rural area where no more than one or two doctors practice in the relevant specialty in the vicinity).

(c) If the opinions of the employee's and the employer's designated health care providers differ, the employer may require the employee to obtain certification from a third health care provider, again at the employer's expense. This third opinion shall be final and binding. The third health care provider must be designated or approved jointly by the employer and the employee. The employer and the employee must each act in good faith to attempt to reach agreement on whom to select for the third opinion provider. If the employer does not attempt in good faith to reach agreement, the employer will be bound by the first certification. If the employee does not attempt in good faith to reach agreement, the employee will be bound by the second certification. For example, an employee who refuses to agree to see a doctor in the specialty in question may be failing to act in good faith. On the other hand, an employer that refuses to agree to any doctor on a list of specialists in the appropriate field provided by the employee and whom the employee has not previously consulted may be failing to act in good faith.

(d) The employer is required to provide the employee with a copy of the second and third medical opinions, where applicable, upon request by the employee. Requested copies are to be provided within two business days unless extenuating circumstances prevent such action.

(e) If the employer requires the employee to obtain either a second or third opinion the employer must reimburse an employee or family member for any reasonable "out of pocket" travel expenses incurred to obtain the second and third medical opinions. The employer may not require the employee or family member to travel outside normal commuting distance for purposes of obtaining the second or third medical opinions except in very unusual circumstances.

(f) In circumstances when the employee or a family member is visiting in another country, or a family member resides in another country, and a serious health condition develops, the employer shall accept a medical certification as well as second and third opinions from a health care provider who practices in that country.

§ 825.308 Under what circumstances may an employer request subsequent recertifications of medical conditions?

(a) For pregnancy, chronic, or permanent/long-term conditions under continuing supervision of a health care provider (as defined in § 825.114(a)(2)(ii), (iii) or (iv)), an employer may request recertification no more often than every 30 days and only in connection with an absence by the employee, unless:

(1) Circumstances described by the previous certification have changed significantly (*e.g.*, the duration or frequency of absences, the severity of the condition, complications); or

(2) The employer receives information that casts doubt upon the employee's stated reason for the absence.

(b)(1) If the minimum duration of the period of incapacity specified on a certification furnished by the health care provider is more than 30 days, the employer may not request recertification until that minimum duration has passed unless one of the conditions set forth in paragraph (c)(1), (2) or (3) of this section is met.

(2) For FMLA leave taken intermittently or on a reduced leave schedule basis, the employer may not request recertification in less than the minimum period specified on the certification as necessary for such leave (including treatment) unless one of the conditions set forth in paragraph (c)(1), (2) or (3) of this section is met.

(c) For circumstances not covered by paragraphs (a) or (b) of this section, an employer may request recertification at any reasonable interval, but not more often than every 30 days, unless:

(1) The employee requests an extension of leave;

(2) Circumstances described by the previous certification have changed significantly (*e.g.*, the duration of the illness, the nature of the illness, complications); or

(3) The employer receives information that casts doubt upon the continuing validity of the certification.

(d) The employee must provide the requested recertification to the employer within the time frame requested by the employer (which must allow at least 15 calendar days after the employer's request), unless it is not practicable under the particular circumstances to do so despite the employee's diligent, good faith efforts.

(e) Any recertification requested by the employer shall be at the employee's expense unless the employer provides otherwise. No second or third opinion on recertification may be required.

§ 825.309 What notice may an employer require regarding an employee's intent to return to work?

(a) An employer may require an employee on FMLA leave to report periodically on the employee's status and intent to return to work. The employer's policy regarding such reports may not be discriminatory and must take into account all of the relevant facts and circumstances related to the individual employee's leave situation.

(b) If an employee gives unequivocal notice of intent not to return to work, the employer's obligations under FMLA to maintain health benefits (subject to COBRA requirements) and to restore the employee cease. However, these obligations continue if an employee indicates he or she may be unable to return to work but expresses a continuing desire to do so.

(c) It may be necessary for an employee to take more leave than originally anticipated. Conversely, an employee may discover after beginning leave that the circumstances have changed and the amount of leave originally anticipated is no longer necessary. An employee may not be required to take more FMLA leave than necessary to resolve the circumstance that precipitated the need for leave. In both of these situations, the employer may require that the employee provide the employer reasonable notice (*i.e.*,within two business days) of the changed circumstances where foreseeable. The employer may also obtain information on such changed circumstances through requested status reports.

§ 825.310 Under what circumstances may an employer require that an employee submit a medical certification that the employee is able (or unable) to return to work (*i.e.*, a "fitness-for- duty" report)?

(a) As a condition of restoring an employee whose FMLA leave was occasioned by the employee's own serious health condition that made the employee unable to perform the employee's job, an employer may have a uniformly-applied policy or practice that requires all similarly-situated employees (*i.e.*, same occupation, same serious health condition) who take leave for such conditions to obtain and present certification from the employee's health care provider that the employee is able to resume work.

(b) If State or local law or the terms of a collective bargaining agreement govern an employee's return to work, those provisions shall be applied. Similarly, requirements under the Americans with Disabilities Act (ADA) that any return-to-work physical be job-related and consistent with business necessity apply. For example, an attorney could not be required to submit to a medical examination or inquiry just because her leg had been amputated. The essential functions of an attorney's job do not require use of both legs; therefore such an inquiry would not be job related. An employer may require a warehouse laborer, whose back impairment affects the ability to lift, to be examined by an orthopedist, but may not require this employee to submit to an HIV test where the test is not related to either the essential functions of his/her job or to his/her impairment.

(c) An employer may seek fitness-for-duty certification only with regard to the particular health condition that caused the employee's need for FMLA leave. The certification itself need only be a simple statement of an employee's ability to return to work. A health care provider employed by the employer may contact the employee's health care provider with the employee's permission, for purposes of clarification of the employee's fitness to return to work. No additional information may be acquired, and clarification may be requested only for the serious health condition for which FMLA leave was taken. The employer may not delay the employee's return to work while contact with the health care provider is being made.

(d) The cost of the certification shall be borne by the employee and the employee is not entitled to be paid for the time or travel costs spent in acquiring the certification.

(e) The notice that employers are required to give to each employee giving notice of the need for FMLA leave regarding their FMLA rights and obligations (*see* § 825.301) shall advise the employee if the employer will require fitness-for-duty certification to return to work. If the employer has a handbook explaining employment policies and benefits, the handbook should explain the employer's general policy regarding any requirement for fitness-for-duty certification to return to work. Specific notice shall also be given to any employee from whom fitness-for-duty certification will be required either at the time notice of the need for leave is given or immediately after leave commences and the employer is advised of the medical circumstances requiring the leave, unless the employee's condition changes from one that did not previously require certification pursuant to the employer's practice or policy. No second or third fitness-for duty certification may be required.

(f) An employer may delay restoration to employment until an employee submits a required fitness-for-duty certification unless the employer has failed to provide the notices required in paragraph (e) of this section.

(g) An employer is not entitled to certification of fitness to return to duty when the employee takes intermittent leave as described in § 825.203.

(h) When an employee is unable to return to work after FMLA leave because of the continuation, recurrence, or onset of the employee's or family member's serious health condition, thereby preventing the employer from recovering its share of health benefit premium payments made on the employee's behalf during a period of unpaid FMLA leave, the employer may require medical certification of the employee's or the family member's serious health condition. (*See* § 825.213(a)(3).) The cost of the certification shall be borne by the employee and the employee is not entitled to be paid for the time or travel costs spent in acquiring the certification.

§ 825.311 What happens if an employee fails to satisfy the medical certification and/or recertification requirements?

(a) In the case of foreseeable leave, an employer may delay the taking of FMLA leave to an employee who fails to provide timely certification after being requested by the employer to furnish such certification (*i.e.*, within 15 calendar days, if practicable), until the required certification is provided.

(b) When the need for leave is *not* foreseeable, or in the case of recertification, an employee must provide certification (or recertification) within the time frame requested by the employer (which must allow at least 15 days after the employer's request) *or* as soon as reasonably possible under the particular facts and circumstances. In the case of a medical emergency, it may not be practicable for an employee to provide the required certification within 15 calendar days. If an employee fails to provide a medical certification within a reasonable time under the pertinent circumstances, the employer may delay the employee's continuation of FMLA leave. If the employee never produces the certification, the leave is not FMLA leave.

(c) When requested by the employer pursuant to a uniformly applied policy for similarly-situated employees, the employee must provide medical certification at the time the employee seeks reinstatement at the end of FMLA leave taken for the employee's serious health condition, that the employee is fit for duty and able to return to work (*see* § 825.310(a)) if the employer has provided the required notice (*see* § 825.301(c); the employer may delay restoration until the certification is provided. In this situation, unless the employee provides either a fitness for-duty certification or a new medical certification for a serious health condition at the time FMLA leave is concluded, the employee may be terminated. *See also* § 825.213(a)(3).

§ 825.312 Under what circumstances may a covered employer refuse to provide FMLA leave or reinstatement to eligible employees?

(a) If an employee fails to give timely advance notice when the need for FMLA leave is foreseeable, the employer may delay the taking of FMLA leave until 30 days after the date the employee provides notice to the employer of the need for FMLA leave. (*See* § 825.302.)

(b) If an employee fails to provide in a timely manner a requested medical certification to substantiate the need for FMLA leave due to a serious health condition, an employer may delay continuation of FMLA leave until an employee submits the certificate. (*See* §§ 825.305 and 825.311.) If the employee never produces the certification, the leave is not FMLA leave.

(c) If an employee fails to provide a requested fitness-for duty certification to return to work, an employer may delay restoration until the employee submits the certificate. (*See* §§ 825.310 and 825.311.)

(d) An employee has no greater right to reinstatement or to other benefits and conditions of employment than if the employee had been continuously employed during the FMLA leave period. Thus, an employee's rights to continued leave, maintenance of health benefits, and restoration cease under FMLA if and when the employment relationship terminates (*e.g.*, layoff), unless that relationship continues, for example, by the employee remaining on *paid* FMLA leave. If the employee is recalled or otherwise re-employed, an eligible employee is immediately entitled to further FMLA leave for an FMLA-qualifying reason. An employer must be able to show, when an employee requests restoration, that the employee would not otherwise have been employed if leave had not been taken in order to deny restoration to employment. (*See* § 825.216.)

(e) An employer may require an employee on FMLA leave to report periodically on the employee's status and intention to return to work. (*See* § 825.309.) If an employee unequivocally advises the employer either before or during the taking of leave that the employee does not intend to return to work, and the employment relationship is terminated, the employee's entitlement to continued leave, maintenance of health benefits, and restoration ceases unless the employment relationship continues, for example, by the employee remaining on *paid* leave. An employee may not be required to take more leave than necessary to address the circumstances for which leave was taken. If the employee is able to return to work earlier than anticipated, the employee shall provide the employer two business days notice where feasible; the employer is required to restore the employee once such notice is given, or where such prior notice was not feasible.

(f) An employer may deny restoration to employment, but not the taking of FMLA leave and the maintenance of health benefits, to an eligible employee only under the terms of the "key employee" exemption. Denial of reinstatement must be necessary to prevent "substantial and grievous economic injury" to the employer's operations. The employer must notify the employee of the employee's status as a "key employee" and of the employer's intent to deny reinstatement on that basis when the employer makes these determinations. If leave has started, the employee must be given a reasonable opportunity to return to work after being so notified. (*See* § 825.219.)

(g) An employee who fraudulently obtains FMLA leave from an employer is not protected by FMLA's job restoration or maintenance of health benefits provisions.

(h) If the employer has a uniformly-applied policy governing outside or supplemental employment, such a policy may continue to apply to an employee while on FMLA leave. An employer which does not have such a policy may not deny benefits to which an employee is entitled under FMLA on this basis unless the FMLA leave was fraudulently obtained as in paragraph (g) of this section.

SUBPART D
What enforcement mechanisms does FMLA provide?

§ 825.400 What can employees do who believe that their rights under FMLA have been violated?

(a) The employee has the choice of:

(1) Filing, or having another person file on his or her behalf, a complaint with the Secretary of Labor, or

(2) Filing a private lawsuit pursuant to section 107 of FMLA.

(b) If the employee files a private lawsuit, it must be filed within two years after the last action which the employee contends was in violation of the Act, or three years if the violation was willful.

(c) If an employer has violated one or more provisions of FMLA, and if justified by the facts of a particular case, an employee may receive one or more of the following: wages, employment benefits, or other compensation denied or lost to such employee by reason of the violation; or, where no such tangible loss has occurred, such as when FMLA leave was unlawfully denied, any actual monetary loss sustained by the employee as a direct result of the violation, such as the cost of providing care, up to a sum equal to 12 weeks of wages for the employee. In addition, the employee may be entitled to interest on such sum, calculated at the prevailing rate. An amount equalling the preceding sums may also be awarded as liquidated damages unless such amount is reduced by the court because the violation was in good faith and the employer had reasonable grounds for believing the employer had not violated the Act. When appropriate, the employee may also obtain appropriate equitable relief, such as employment, reinstatement and promotion. When the employer is found in violation, the employee may recover a reasonable attorney's fee, reasonable expert witness fees, and other costs of the action from the employer in addition to any judgment awarded by the court.

§ 825.401 Where may an employee file a complaint of FMLA violations with the Federal government?

(a) A complaint may be filed in person, by mail or by telephone, with the Wage and Hour Division, Employment Standards Administration, U.S. Department of Labor. A complaint may be filed at any local office of the Wage and Hour Division; the address and telephone number of local offices may be found in telephone directories.

(b) A complaint filed with the Secretary of Labor should be filed within a reasonable time of when the employee discovers that his or her FMLA rights have been violated. In no event may a complaint be filed more than two years after the action which is alleged to be a violation of FMLA occurred, or three years in the case of a willful violation.

(c) No particular form of complaint is required, except that a complaint must be reduced to writing and should include a full statement of the acts and/or omissions, with pertinent dates, which are believed to constitute the violation.

§ 825.402 How is an employer notified of a violation of the posting requirement?

Section 825.300 describes the requirements for covered employers to post a notice for employees that explains the Act's provisions. If a representative of the Department of Labor determines that an employer has committed a willful violation of this posting requirement, and that the imposition of a civil money penalty for such violation is appropriate, the representative may issue and serve a notice of penalty on such employer in person or by certified mail. Where service by certified mail is not accepted, notice shall be deemed received on the date of attempted delivery. Where service is not accepted, the notice may be served by regular mail.

§ 825.403 How may an employer appeal the assessment of a penalty for willful violation of the posting requirement?

(a) An employer may obtain a review of the assessment of penalty from the Wage and Hour Regional Administrator for the region in which the alleged violation(s) occurred. If the employer does not seek such a review or fails to do so in a timely manner, the notice of the penalty constitutes the final ruling of the Secretary of Labor.

(b) To obtain review, an employer may file a petition with the Wage and Hour Regional Administrator for the region in which the alleged violations occurred. No particular form of petition for review is required, except that the petition must be in writing, should contain the legal and factual bases for the petition, and must be mailed to the Regional Administrator within 15 days of receipt of the notice of penalty. The employer may request an oral hearing which may be conducted by telephone.

(c) The decision of the Regional Administrator constitutes the final order of the Secretary.

§ 825.404 What are the consequences of an employer not paying the penalty assessment after a final order is issued?

The Regional Administrator may seek to recover the unpaid penalty pursuant to the Debt Collection Act (DCA), 31 U.S.C. 3711 *et seq.*, and, in addition to seeking recovery of the unpaid final order, may seek interest and penalties as provided under the DCA. The final order may also be referred to the

Solicitor of Labor for collection. The Secretary may file suit in any court of competent jurisdiction to recover the monies due as a result of the unpaid final order, interest, and penalties.

SUBPART E
What records must be kept to comply with the FMLA?

§ 825.500 What records must an employer keep to comply with the FMLA?

(a) FMLA provides that covered employers shall make, keep, and preserve records pertaining to their obligations under the Act in accordance with the recordkeeping requirements of section 11(c) of the Fair Labor Standards Act (FLSA) and in accordance with these regulations. FMLA also restricts the authority of the Department of Labor to require any employer or plan, fund or program to submit books or records more than once during any 12-month period unless the Department has reasonable cause to believe a violation of the FMLA exists or the DOL is investigating a complaint. These regulations establish no requirement for the submission of any records unless specifically requested by a Departmental official.

(b) *Form of records.* No particular order or form of records is required. These regulations establish no requirement that any employer revise its computerized payroll or personnel records systems to comply. However, employers must keep the records specified by these regulations for no less than three years and make them available for inspection, copying, and transcription by representatives of the Department of Labor upon request. The records may be maintained and preserved on microfilm or other basic source document of an automated data processing memory provided that adequate projection or viewing equipment is available, that the reproductions are clear and identifiable by date or pay period, and that extensions or transcriptions of the information required herein can be and are made available upon request. Records kept in computer form must be made available for transcription or copying.

(c) *Items required.* Covered employers who have eligible employees must maintain records that must disclose the following:

(1) Basic payroll and identifying employee data, including name, address, and occupation; rate or basis of pay and terms of compensation; daily and weekly hours worked per pay period; additions to or deductions from wages; and total compensation paid.

(2) Dates FMLA leave is taken by FMLA eligible employees (*e.g.*, available from time records, requests for leave, *etc.*, if so designated). Leave must be designated in records as FMLA leave; leave so designated may not

include leave required under State law or an employer plan which is not also covered by FMLA.

(3) If FMLA leave is taken by eligible employees in increments of less than one full day, the hours of the leave.

(4) Copies of employee notices of leave furnished to the employer under FMLA, if in writing, and copies of all general and specific written notices given to employees as required under FMLA and these regulations (*see* § 825.301(b)). Copies may be maintained in employee personnel files.

(5) Any documents (including written and electronic records) describing employee benefits or employer policies and practices regarding the taking of paid and unpaid leaves.

(6) Premium payments of employee benefits.

(7) Records of any dispute between the employer and an eligible employee regarding designation of leave as FMLA leave, including any written statement from the employer or employee of the reasons for the designation and for the disagreement.

(d) Covered employers with no eligible employees must maintain the records set forth in paragraph (c)(1) above.

(e) Covered employers in a joint employment situation (*see* § 825.106) must keep all the records required by paragraph (c) of this section with respect to any primary employees, and must keep the records required by paragraph (c)(1) with respect to any secondary employees.

(f) If FMLA-eligible employees are not subject to FLSA's recordkeeping regulations for purposes of minimum wage or overtime compliance (*i.e.*, not covered by or exempt from FLSA), an employer need not keep a record of actual hours worked (as otherwise required under FLSA, 29 CFR 516.2(a)(7)), provided that:

(1) eligibility for FMLA leave is presumed for any employee who has been employed for at least 12 months; and

(2) with respect to employees who take FMLA leave intermittently or on a reduced leave schedule, the employer and employee agree on the employee's normal schedule or average hours worked each week and reduce their agreement to a written record maintained in accordance with paragraph (b) of this section.

(g) Records and documents relating to medical certifications, recertifications or medical histories of employees or employees' family members, created for purposes of FMLA, shall be maintained as confidential medical records in separate files/records from the usual personnel files, and if ADA is also applicable, such records shall be maintained in conformance with ADA confidentiality requirements (*see* 29 CFR § 1630.14(c)(1)), except that:

(1) Supervisors and managers may be informed regarding necessary restrictions on the work or duties of an employee and necessary accommodations;

(2) First aid and safety personnel may be informed (when appropriate) if the employee's physical or medical condition might require emergency treatment; and

(3) Government officials investigating compliance with FMLA (or other pertinent law) shall be provided relevant information upon request.

SUBPART F
What special rules apply to employees of schools?

§ 825.600 To whom do the special rules apply?

(a) Certain special rules apply to employees of "local educational agencies," including public school boards and elementary and secondary schools under their jurisdiction, and private elementary and secondary schools. The special rules do not apply to other kinds of educational institutions, such as colleges and universities, trade schools, and preschools.

(b) Educational institutions are covered by FMLA (and these special rules) and the Act's 50-employee coverage test does not apply. The usual requirements for employees to be "eligible" do apply, however, including employment at a worksite where at least 50 employees are employed within 75 miles. For example, employees of a rural school would not be eligible for FMLA leave if the school has fewer than 50 employees and there are no other schools under the jurisdiction of the same employer (usually, a school board) within 75 miles.

(c) The special rules affect the taking of intermittent leave or leave on a reduced leave schedule, or leave near the end of an academic term (semester), by instructional employees. "Instructional employees" are those whose principal function is to teach and instruct students in a class, a small group, or an individual setting. This term includes not only teachers, but also athletic coaches, driving instructors, and special education assistants such as signers for the hearing impaired. It does not include, and the special rules do not apply to, teacher assistants or aides who do not have as their principal job actual teaching or instructing, nor does it include auxiliary personnel such as counselors, psychologists, or curriculum specialists. It also does not include cafeteria workers, maintenance workers, or bus drivers.

(d) Special rules which apply to restoration to an equivalent position apply to all employees of local educational agencies.

§ 825.601 What limitations apply to the taking of intermittent leave or leave on a reduced leave schedule?

(a) Leave taken for a period that ends with the school year and begins the next semester is leave taken consecutively rather than intermittently. The period during the summer vacation when the employee would not have been required to report for duty is not counted against the employee's FMLA leave entitlement. An instructional employee who is on FMLA leave at the end of the school year must be provided with any benefits over the summer vacation that employees would normally receive if they had been working at the end of the school year.

(1) If an eligible instructional employee needs intermittent leave or leave on a reduced leave schedule to care for a family member, or for the employee's own serious health condition, which is foreseeable based on planned medical treatment, and the employee would be on leave for more than 20 percent of the total number of working days over the period the leave would extend, the employer may require the employee to choose either to:

(i) Take leave for a period or periods of a particular duration, not greater than the duration of the planned treatment; or

(ii) Transfer temporarily to an available alternative position for which the employee is qualified, which has equivalent pay and benefits and which better accommodates recurring periods of leave than does the employee's regular position.

(2) These rules apply only to a leave involving more than 20 percent of the working days during the period over which the leave extends. For example, if an instructional employee who normally works five days each week needs to take two days of FMLA leave per week over a period of several weeks, the special rules would apply. Employees taking leave which constitutes 20 percent or less of the working days during the leave period would not be subject to transfer to an alternative position. "Periods of a particular duration" means a block, or blocks, of time beginning no earlier than the first day for which leave is needed and ending no later than the last day on which leave is needed, and may include one uninterrupted period of leave.

(b) If an instructional employee does not give required notice of foreseeable FMLA leave (*see* § 825.302) to be taken intermittently or on a reduced leave schedule, the employer may require the employee to take leave of a particular duration, or to transfer temporarily to an alternative position. Alternatively, the employer may require the employee to delay the taking of leave until the notice provision is met. *See* § 825.207(h).

§ 825.602 What limitations apply to the taking of leave near the end of an academic term?

(a) There are also different rules for instructional employees who begin leave more than five weeks before the end of a term, less than five weeks before the end of a term, and less than three weeks before the end of a term. Regular rules apply except in circumstances when:

(1) An instructional employee begins leave more than five weeks before the end of a term. The employer may require the employee to continue taking leave until the end of the term if-

(i) The leave will last at least three weeks, and

(ii) The employee would return to work during the three-week period before the end of the term.

(2) The employee begins leave for a purpose other than the employee's own serious health condition *during* the five-week period before the end of a term. The employer may require the employee to continue taking leave until the end of the term if-

(i) The leave will last more than two weeks, and

(ii) The employee would return to work during the two-week period before the end of the term.

(3) The employee begins leave for a purpose other than the employee's own serious health condition during the three-week period before the end of a term, and the leave will last more than five working days. The employer may require the employee to continue taking leave until the end of the term.

(b) For purposes of these provisions, "academic term" means the school semester, which typically ends near the end of the calendar year and the end of spring each school year. In no case may a school have more than two academic terms or semesters each year for purposes of FMLA. An example of leave falling within these provisions would be where an employee plans two weeks of leave to care for a family member which will begin three weeks before the end of the term. In that situation, the employer could require the employee to stay out on leave until the end of the term.

§ 825.603 Is all leave taken during "periods of a particular duration" counted against the FMLA leave entitlement?

(a) If an employee chooses to take leave for "periods of a particular duration" in the case of intermittent or reduced schedule leave, the entire period of leave taken will count as FMLA leave.

(b) In the case of an employee who is required to take leave until the end of an academic term, only the period of leave until the employee is ready and able to return to work shall be charged against the employee's FMLA leave entitlement. The employer has the option not to require the employee to stay on leave until the end of the school term. Therefore, any additional leave required by the employer to the end of the school term is not counted as FMLA leave; however, the employer shall be required to maintain the employee's group health insurance and restore the employee to the same or equivalent job including other benefits at the conclusion of the leave.

§ 825.604 What special rules apply to restoration to "an equivalent position?"

The determination of how an employee is to be restored to "an equivalent position" upon return from FMLA leave will be made on the basis of "established school board policies and practices, private school policies and practices, and collective bargaining agreements." The "established policies" and collective bargaining agreements used as a basis for restoration must be in writing, must be made known to the employee prior to the taking of FMLA leave, and must clearly explain the employee's restoration rights upon return from leave. Any established policy which is used as the basis for restoration of an employee to "an equivalent position" must provide substantially the same protections as provided in the Act for reinstated employees. *See* § 825.215. In other words, the policy or collective bargaining agreement must provide for restoration to an "equivalent position" with equivalent employment benefits, pay, and other terms and conditions of employment. For example, an employee may not be restored to a position requiring additional licensure or certification.

SUBPART G
How do other laws, employer practices, and collective bargaining agreements affect employee rights under FMLA?

§ 825.700 What if an employer provides more generous benefits than required by FMLA?

(a) An employer must observe any employment benefit program or plan that provides greater family or medical leave rights to employees than the rights established by the FMLA. Conversely, the rights established by the Act may not be diminished by any employment benefit program or plan. For example, a provision of a CBA which provides for reinstatement to a position that is not equivalent because of seniority (*e.g.*, provides lesser pay) is superseded by FMLA. If an employer provides greater unpaid family leave rights than are afforded by FMLA, the employer is not required to extend additional rights afforded by FMLA, such as maintenance of health benefits (other than through COBRA), to the additional leave period not covered by FMLA. If an employee takes paid or unpaid leave and the employer does not designate the leave as FMLA leave, the leave taken does not count against an employee's FMLA entitlement.

(b) Nothing in this Act prevents an employer from amending existing leave and employee benefit programs, provided they comply with FMLA. However, nothing in the Act is intended to discourage employers from adopting or retaining more generous leave policies.

(c) (1) The Act does not apply to employees under a collective bargaining agreement (CBA) in effect on August 5, 1993, until February 5, 1994, or the date the agreement terminates (*i.e.*, its expiration date), whichever is earlier. Thus, if the CBA contains family or medical leave benefits, whether greater or less than those under the Act, such benefits are not disturbed until the Act's provisions begin to apply to employees under that agreement. A CBA which provides no family or medical leave rights also continues in effect. For CBAs subject to the Railway Labor Act and other CBAs which do not have an expiration date for the general terms, but which may be reopened at specified times, *e.g.*, to amend wages and benefits, the first time the agreement is amended after August 5, 1993, shall be considered the termination date of the CBA, and the effective date for FMLA.

(2) As discussed in § 825.102(b), the period prior to the Act's delayed effective date must be considered in determining employer coverage and employee eligibility for FMLA leave.

§ 825.701 Do State laws providing family and medical leave still apply?

(a) Nothing in FMLA supersedes any provision of State or local law that provides greater family or medical leave rights than those provided by FMLA. The Department of Labor will not, however, enforce State family or medical leave laws, and States may not enforce the FMLA. Employees are not required to designate whether the leave they are taking is FMLA leave or leave under State law, and an employer must comply with the appropriate (applicable) provisions of both. An employer covered by one law and not the other has to comply only with the law under which it is covered. Similarly, an employee eligible under only one law must receive benefits in accordance with that law. If leave qualifies for FMLA leave and leave under State law, the leave used counts against the employee's entitlement under both laws. Examples of the interaction between FMLA and State laws include:

(1) If State law provides 16 weeks of leave entitlement over two years, an employee would be entitled to take 16 weeks one year under State law and 12 weeks the next year under FMLA. Health benefits maintenance under FMLA would be applicable only to the first 12 weeks of leave entitlement each year. If the employee took 12 weeks the first year, the employee would be entitled to a maximum of 12 weeks the second year under FMLA (not 16 weeks). An employee would not be entitled to 28 weeks in one year.

(2) If State law provides half-pay for employees temporarily disabled because of pregnancy for six weeks, the employee would be entitled to an additional six weeks of unpaid FMLA leave (or accrued paid leave).

(3) A shorter notice period under State law must be allowed by the employer unless an employer has already provided, or the employee is requesting, more leave than required under State law.

(4) If State law provides for only one medical certification, no additional certifications may be required by the employer unless the employer has

already provided, or the employee is requesting, more leave than required under State law.

(5) If State law provides six weeks of leave, which may include leave to care for a seriously-ill grandparent or a "spouse equivalent," and leave was used for that purpose, the employee is still entitled to 12 weeks of FMLA leave, as the leave used was provided for a purpose not covered by FMLA. If FMLA leave is used first for a purpose also provided under State law, and State leave has thereby been exhausted, the employer would not be required to provide additional leave to care for the grandparent or "spouse equivalent."

(6) If State law prohibits mandatory leave beyond the actual period of pregnancy disability, an instructional employee of an educational agency subject to special FMLA rules may not be required to remain on leave until the end of the academic term, as permitted by FMLA under certain circumstances. (*See* Subpart F of this part.)

§ 825.702 How does FMLA affect Federal and State anti-discrimination laws?

(a) Nothing in FMLA modifies or affects any Federal or State law prohibiting discrimination on the basis of race, religion, color, national origin, sex, age, or disability (*e.g.*, Title VII of the Civil Rights Act of 1964, as amended by the Pregnancy Discrimination Act). FMLA's legislative history explains that FMLA is "not intended to modify or affect the Rehabilitation Act of 1973, as amended, the regulations concerning employment which have been promulgated pursuant to that statute, or the Americans with Disabilities Act of 1990, or the regulations issued under that act. Thus, the leave provisions of the [FMLA] are wholly distinct from the reasonable accommodation obligations of employers covered under the [ADA], employers who receive Federal financial assistance, employers who contract with the Federal government, or the Federal government itself. The purpose of the FMLA is to make leave available to eligible employees and employers within its coverage, and not to limit already existing rights and protection." S. Rep. No. 3, 103d Cong., 1st Sess. 38 (1993). An employer must therefore provide leave under whichever statutory provision provides the greater rights to employees. When an employer violates both FMLA and a discrimination law, an employee may be able to recover under either or both statutes (double relief may not be awarded for the same loss; when remedies coincide a claimant may be allowed to utilize whichever avenue of relief is desired (*Laffey v. Northwest Airlines, Inc.*, 567 F.2d 429, 445 (D.C. Cir. 1976), *cert. denied*, 434 U.S. 1086 (1978))).

(b) If an employee is a qualified individual with a disability within the meaning of the Americans with Disabilities Act (ADA), the employer must make reasonable accommodations, *etc.*, barring undue hardship, in accordance with the ADA. At the same time, the employer must afford an employee his or her FMLA rights. ADA's "disability" and FMLA's "serious health condition" are different concepts, and must be analyzed separately. FMLA entitles eligible employees to 12 weeks of leave in any 12-month period, whereas the ADA allows an indeterminate amount of leave, barring undue hardship, as a reasonable accommodation. FMLA requires employers to maintain employees' group health plan coverage during FMLA leave on the same conditions as coverage would have been provided if the employee had been continuously employed during the leave period, whereas ADA does not require maintenance of health insurance unless other employees receive health insurance during leave under the same circumstances.

(c)(1) A reasonable accommodation under the ADA might be accomplished by providing an individual with a disability with a part-time job with no health benefits, assuming the employer did not ordinarily provide health insurance for part-time employees. However, FMLA would permit an employee to work a reduced leave schedule until the equivalent of 12 workweeks of leave were used, with group health benefits maintained during this period. FMLA permits an employer to temporarily transfer an employee who istaking leave intermittently or on a reduced leave schedule to an alternative position, whereas the ADA allows an accommodation of reassignment to an equivalent, vacant position only if the employee cannot perform the essential functions of the employee's present position and an accommodation is not possible in the employee's present position, or an accommodation in the employee's present position would cause an undue hardship. The examples in the following paragraphs of this section demonstrate how the two laws would interact with respect to a qualified individual with a disability.

(2) A qualified individual with a disability who is also an "eligible employee" entitled to FMLA leave requests 10 weeks of medical leave as a reasonable accommodation, which the employer grants because it is not an undue hardship. The employer advises the employee that the 10 weeks of leave is also being designated as FMLA leave and will count towards the employee's FMLA leave entitlement. This designation does not prevent the parties from also treating the leave as a reasonable accommodation and reinstating the employee into the *same* job, as required by the ADA, rather than an equivalent position under FMLA, if that is the greater right available to the employee. At the same time, the employee would be entitled under FMLA to have the employer maintain group health plan coverage during the leave, as that requirement provides the greater right to the employee.

(3) If the same employee needed to work part-time (a reduced leave schedule) after returning to his or her same job, the employee would still be entitled under FMLA to have group health plan coverage maintained for the

remainder of the two-week equivalent of FMLA leave entitlement, notwith-standing an employer policy that part-time employees do not receive health insurance. This employee would be entitled under the ADA to reasonable accommodations to enable the employee to perform the essential functions of the part-time position. In addition, because the employee is working a part-time schedule as a reasonable accommodation, the employee would be shielded from FMLA's provision for temporary assignment to a different alternative position. Once the employee has exhausted his or her remaining FMLA leave entitlement while working the reduced (part-time) schedule, if the employee is a qualified individual with a disability, and if the employee is unable to return to the same full-time position at that time, the employee might continue to work part-time as a reasonable accommodation, barring undue hardship; the employee would then be entitled to only those employ-ment benefits ordinarily provided by the employer to part-time employees.

(4) At the end of the FMLA leave entitlement, an employer is required under FMLA to reinstate the employee in the same or an equivalent posi-tion, with equivalent pay and benefits, to that which the employee held when leave commenced. The employer's FMLA obligations would be satis-fied if the employer offered the employee an equivalent full-time position. If the employee were unable to perform the essential functions of that equiva-lent position even with reasonable accommodation, because of a disability, the ADA may require the employer to make a reasonable accommodation at that time by allowing the employee to work part-time or by reassigning the employee to a vacant position, barring undue hardship.

(d)(1) If FMLA entitles an employee to leave, an employer may not, in lieu of FMLA leave entitlement, *require* an employee to take a job with a reasonable accommodation. However, ADA may require that an employer offer an employee the opportunity to take such a position. An employer may not change the essential functions of the job in order to deny FMLA leave. *See* § 825.220(b).

(2) An employee may be on a workers' compensation absence due to an on-the-job injury or illness which also qualifies as a serious health condition under FMLA. The workers' compensation absence and FMLA leave may run concurrently (subject to proper notice and designation by the employ-er). At some point the health care provider providing medical care pursuant to the workers' compensation injury may certify the employee is able to return to work in a "light duty" position. If the employer offers such a posi-tion, the employee is permitted but not required to accept the position (*see* § 825.220(d)). As a result, the employee may no longer qualify for payments from the workers' compensation benefit plan, but the employee is entitled to continue on unpaid FMLA leave either until the employee is able to return to the same or equivalent job the employee left or until the 12-week FMLA leave entitlement is exhausted. *See* § 825.207(d)(2). If the employee

returning from the workers' compensation injury is a qualified individual with a disability, he or she will have rights under the ADA.

(e) If an employer requires certifications of an employee's fitness for duty to return to work, as permitted by FMLA under a uniform policy, it must comply with the ADA requirement that a fitness for duty physical be job-related and consistent with business necessity.

(f) Under Title VII of the Civil Rights Act of 1964, as amended by the Pregnancy Discrimination Act, an employer should provide the same benefits for women who are pregnant as the employer provides to other employees with short-term disabilities. Because Title VII does not require employees to be employed for a certain period of time to be protected, an employee employed for less than 12 months by the employer (and, therefore, not an "eligible" employee under FMLA) may *not* be denied maternity leave if the employer normally provides short-term disability benefits to employees with the same tenure who are experiencing other short term disabilities.

(g) For further information on Federal antidiscrimination laws, including Title VII and the ADA, individuals are encouraged to contact the nearest office of the U.S. Equal Employment Opportunity Commission.

SUBPART H
Definitions

§ 825.800 Definitions.

For purposes of this part:

Act or *FMLA* means the Family and Medical Leave Act of 1993, Public Law 103-3 (February 5, 1993), 107 Stat. 6 (29 U.S.C. 2601 *et seq.*)

ADA means the Americans With Disabilities Act (42 USC 12101 *et seq.*)

Administrator means the Administrator of the Wage and Hour Division, Employment Standards Administration, U.S. Department of Labor, and includes any official of the Wage and Hour Division authorized to perform any of the functions of the Administrator under this part.

COBRA means the continuation coverage requirements of Title X of the Consolidated Omnibus Budget Reconciliation Act of 1986, As Amended (Pub.L. 99-272, title X, section 10002; 100 Stat 227; 29 U.S.C. 1161 -1168).

Commerce and industry or activity affecting commerce mean any activity, business, or industry in commerce or in which a labor dispute would hinder or obstruct commerce or the free flow of commerce, and include "commerce" and any "industry affecting commerce" as defined in sections 501(1) and 501(3) of the Labor Management Relations Act of 1947, 29 U.S.C. 142(1) and (3).

Continuing treatment means: A serious health condition involving continuing treatment by a health care provider includes any one or more of the following:

(1) A period of *incapacity* (*i.e.*, inability to work, attend school or perform other regular daily activities due to the serious health condition, treatment therefor, or recovery therefrom) of more than three consecutive calendar days, and any subsequent treatment or period of incapacity relating to the same condition, that also involves:

(i) Treatment two or more times by a health care provider, by a nurse or physician's assistant under direct supervision of a health care provider, or by a provider of health care services (*e.g.*, physical therapist) under orders of, or on referral by, a health care provider; or

(ii) Treatment by a health care provider on at least one occasion which results in a regimen of continuing treatment under the supervision of the health care provider.

(2) Any period of incapacity due to pregnancy, or for prenatal care.

(3) Any period of incapacity or treatment for such incapacity due to a chronic serious health condition. A chronic serious health condition is one which:

(i) Requires periodic visits for treatment by a health care provider, or by a nurse or physician's assistant under direct supervision of a health care provider;

(ii) Continues over an extended period of time (including recurring episodes of a single underlying condition); and

(iii) May cause episodic rather than a continuing period of incapacity (*e.g.*, asthma, diabetes, epilepsy, *etc.*).

(4) A period of incapacity which is permanent or long-term due to a condition for which treatment may not be effective. The employee or family member must be under the continuing supervision of, but need not be receiving active treatment by, a health care provider. Examples include Alzheimer's, a severe stroke, or the terminal stages of a disease.

(5) Any period of absence to receive multiple treatments (including any period of recovery therefrom) by a health care provider or by a provider of health care services under orders of, or on referral by, a health care provider, either for restorative surgery after an accident or other injury, or for a condition that would likely result in a period of incapacity of more than three consecutive calendar days in the absence of medical intervention or treatment, such as cancer (chemotherapy, radiation, *etc.*), severe arthritis (physical therapy), kidney disease (dialysis).

Eligible employee means:

(1) An employee who has been employed for a total of at least 12 months by the employer on the date on which any FMLA leave is to commence; and

(2) Who, on the date on which any FMLA leave is to commence, has been employed for at least 1,250 hours of service with such employer during the previous 12-month period; and

(3) Who is employed in any State of the United States, the District of Columbia or any Territories or possession of the United States.

(4) Excludes any Federal officer or employee covered under subchapter V of chapter 63 of title 5, United States Code; and

(5) Excludes any employee of the U.S. Senate or the U.S. House of Representatives covered under title V of the FMLA; and

(6) Excludes any employee who is employed at a worksite at which the employer employs fewer than 50 employees if the total number of employees employed by that employer within 75 miles of that worksite is also fewer than 50.

(7) Excludes any employee employed in any country other than the United States or any Territory or possession of the United States.

Employ means to suffer or permit to work.

Employee has the meaning given the same term as defined in section 3(e) of the Fair Labor Standards Act, 29 U.S.C. 203(e), as follows:

(1) The term "employee" means any individual employed by an employer;

(2) In the case of an individual employed by a public agency, "employee" means:

(i) Any individual employed by the Government of the United States-

(A) As a civilian in the military departments (as defined in section 102 of Title 5, United States Code),

(B) In any executive agency (as defined in section 105 of Title 5, United States Code), excluding any Federal officer or employee covered under subchapter V of chapter 63 of Title 5, United States Code,

(C) In any unit of the legislative or judicial branch of the Government which has positions in the competitive service, excluding any employee of the U.S. Senate or U.S. House of Representatives who is covered under Title V of FMLA,

(D) In a nonappropriated fund instrumentality under the jurisdiction of the Armed Forces, or

(ii) Any individual employed by the United States Postal Service or the Postal Rate Commission; and

(iii) Any individual employed by a State, political subdivision of a State, or an interstate governmental agency, other than such an individual-

(A) Who is not subject to the civil service laws of the State, political subdivision, or agency which employs the employee; and

(B) Who:

(1) Holds a public elective office of that State, political subdivision, or agency,

(2) Is selected by the holder of such an office to be a member of his personal staff,

(3) Is appointed by such an officeholder to serve on a policymaking level,

(4) Is an immediate adviser to such an officeholder with respect to the constitutional or legal powers of the office of such officeholder, or

(5) Is an employee in the legislative branch or legislative body of that State, political subdivision, or agency and is not employed by the legislative library of such State, political subdivision, or agency.

Employee employed in an instructional capacity. See *Teacher.*

Employer means any person engaged in commerce or in an industry or activity affecting commerce who employs 50 or more employees for each working day during each of 20 or more calendar workweeks in the current or preceding calendar year, and includes-

(1) Any person who acts, directly or indirectly, in the interest of an employer to any of the employees of such employer;

(2) Any successor in interest of an employer; and

(3) Any public agency.

Employment benefits means all benefits provided or made available to employees by an employer, including group life insurance, health insurance, disability insurance, sick leave, annual leave, educational benefits, and pensions, regardless of whether such benefits are provided by a practice or written policy of an employer or through an "employee benefit plan" as defined in section 3(3) of the Employee Retirement Income Security Act of 1974, 29 U.S.C. 1002(3). The term does not include non-employment related obligations paid by employees through voluntary deductions such as supplemental insurance coverage. (*See* § 825.209(a)).

FLSA means the Fair Labor Standards Act (29 U.S.C. 201 *et seq.*).

Group health plan means any plan of, or contributed to by, an employer (including a self-insured plan) to provide health care (directly or otherwise) to the employer's employees, former employees, or the families of such employees or former employees. For purposes of FMLA the term "group health plan" shall not include an insurance program providing health coverage under which employees purchase individual policies from insurers provided that:

(1) No contributions are made by the employer;

(2) Participation in the program is completely voluntary for employees;

(3) The sole functions of the employer with respect to the program are, without endorsing the program, to permit the insurer to publicize the program to employees, to collect premiums through payroll deductions and to remit them to the insurer;

(4) The employer receives no consideration in the form of cash or otherwise in connection with the program, other than reasonable compensation,

excluding any profit, for administrative services actually rendered in connection with payroll deduction; and,

(5) the premium charged with respect to such coverage does not increase in the event the employment relationship terminates.

Health care provider means:

(1) A doctor of medicine or osteopathy who is authorized to practice medicine or surgery by the State in which the doctor practices; or

(2) Podiatrists, dentists, clinical psychologists, optometrists, and chiropractors (limited to treatment consisting of manual manipulation of the spine to correct a subluxation as demonstrated by X-ray to exist) authorized to practice in the State and performing within the scope of their practice as defined under State law; and

(3) Nurse practitioners, nurse-midwives and clinical social workers who are authorized to practice under State law and who are performing within the scope of their practice as defined under State law; and

(4) Christian Science practitioners listed with the First Church of Christ, Scientist in Boston, Massachusetts.

(5) Any health care provider from whom an employer or a group health plan's benefits manager will accept certification of the existence of a serious health condition to substantiate a claim for benefits.

(6) A health care provider as defined above who practices in a country other than the United States, who is licensed to practice in accordance with the laws and regulations of that country.

"Incapable of self-care" means that the individual requires active assistance or supervision to provide daily self-care in several of the "activities of daily living" (ADLs) or "instrumental activities of daily living" (IADLs). Activities of daily living include adaptive activities such as caring appropriately for one's grooming and hygiene, bathing, dressing and eating. Instrumental activities of daily living include cooking, cleaning, shopping, taking public transportation, paying bills, maintaining a residence, using telephones and directories, using a post office, *etc.*

Instructional employee: See *Teacher.*

Intermittent leave means leave taken in separate periods of time due to a single illness or injury, rather than for one continuous period of time, and may include leave of periods from an hour or more to several weeks. Examples of intermittent leave would include leave taken on an occasional basis for medical appointments, or leave taken several days at a time spread over a period of six months, such as for chemotherapy.

Mental disability: See *Physical or mental disability.*

Parent means the biological parent of an employee or an individual who stands or stood *in loco parentis* to an employee when the employee was a child.

Person means an individual, partnership, association, corporation, business trust, legal representative, or any organized group of persons, and includes a public agency for purposes of this part.

Physical or mental disability means a physical or mental impairment that substantially limits one or more of the major life activities of an individual. Regulations at 29 CFR Part 1630.2(h), (i), and (j), issued by the Equal Employment Opportunity Commission under the Americans with Disabilities Act (ADA), 42 U.S.C. 12101 *et seq.*, define these terms.

Public agency means the government of the United States; the government of a State or political subdivision thereof; any agency of the United States (including the United States Postal Service and Postal Rate Commission), a State, or a political subdivision of a State, or any interstate governmental agency. Under section 101(5)(B) of the Act, a public agency is considered to be a "person" engaged in commerce or in an industry or activity affecting commerce within the meaning of the Act.

Reduced leave schedule means a leave schedule that reduces the usual number of hours per workweek, or hours per workday, of an employee.

Secretary means the Secretary of Labor or authorized representative.

Serious health condition entitling an employee to FMLA leave means:
   (1) an illness, injury, impairment, or physical or mental condition that involves:
      (i) Inpatient care (*i.e.*, an overnight stay) in a hospital, hospice, or residential medical care facility, including any period of incapacity (for purposes of this section, defined to mean inability to work, attend school or perform other regular daily activities due to the serious health condition, treatment therefor, or recovery therefrom), or any subsequent treatment in connection with such inpatient care; or
      (ii) Continuing treatment by a health care provider. A serious health condition involving continuing treatment by a health care provider includes:
         (A) A period of incapacity (*i.e.*, inability to work, attend school or perform other regular daily activities due to the serious health condition, treatment therefore, or recovery therefrom) of more than three consecutive calendar days, including any subsequent treatment or period of incapacity relating to the same condition, that also involves:
            (1) Treatment two or more times by a health care provider, by a nurse or physician's assistant under direct supervision of a health care provider, or by a provider of health care services (*e.g.*, physical therapist) under orders of, or on referral by, a health care provider; or

(2) Treatment by a health care provider on at least one occasion which results in a regimen of continuing treatment under the supervision of the health care provider.

(B) Any period of incapacity due to pregnancy, or for prenatal care.

(C) Any period of incapacity or treatment for such incapacity due to a chronic serious health condition. A chronic serious health condition is one which:

(1) Requires periodic visits for treatment by a health care provider, or by a nurse or physician's assistant under direct supervision of a health care provider;

(2) Continues over an extended period of time (including recurring episodes of a single underlying condition); and

(3) May cause episodic rather than a continuing period of incapacity (*e.g.*, asthma, diabetes, epilepsy, *etc.*).

(D) A period of incapacity which is permanent or long-term due to a condition for which treatment may not be effective. The employee or family member must be under the continuing supervision of, but need not be receiving active treatment by, a health care provider. Examples include Alzheimer's, a severe stroke, or the terminal stages of a disease.

(E) Any period of absence to receive multiple treatments (including any period of recovery therefrom) by a health care provider or by a provider of health care services under orders of, or on referral by, a health care provider, either for restorative surgery after an accident or other injury, or for a condition that would likely result in a period of incapacity of more than three consecutive calendar days in the absence of medical intervention or treatment, such as cancer (chemotherapy, radiation, *etc.*), severe arthritis (physical therapy), kidney disease (dialysis).

(2) Treatment for purposes of paragraph (1) of this definition includes (but is not limited to) examinations to determine if a serious health condition exists and evaluations of the condition. Treatment does not include routine physical examinations, eye examinations, or dental examinations. Under paragraph (1)(ii)(A)(2) of this definition, a regimen of continuing treatment includes, for example, a course of prescription medication (*e.g.*, an antibiotic) or therapy requiring special equipment to resolve or alleviate the health condition (*e.g.*, oxygen). A regimen of continuing treatment that includes the taking of over-the-counter medications such as aspirin, antihistamines, or salves; or bed-rest, drinking fluids, exercise, and other similar activities that can be initiated without a visit to a health care provider, is not, by itself, sufficient to constitute a regimen of continuing treatment for purposes of FMLA leave.

(3) Conditions for which cosmetic treatments are administered (such as most treatments for acne or plastic surgery) are not "serious health condi-

tions" unless inpatient hospital care is required or unless complications develop. Ordinarily, unless complications arise, the common cold, the flu, ear aches, upset stomach, minor ulcers, headaches other than migraine, routine dental or orthodontia problems, periodontal disease, *etc.*, are examples of conditions that do not meet the definition of a serious health condition and do not qualify for FMLA leave. Restorative dental or plastic surgery after an injury or removal of cancerous growths are serious health conditions provided all the other conditions of this regulation are met. Mental illness resulting from stress or allergies may be serious health conditions, but only if all the conditions of this section are met.

(4) Substance abuse may be a serious health condition if the conditions of this section are met. However, FMLA leave may only be taken for treatment for substance abuse by a health care provider or by a provider of health care services on referral by a health care provider. On the other hand, absence because of the employee's use of the substance, rather than for treatment, does not qualify for FMLA leave.

(5) Absences attributable to incapacity under paragraphs (1) (ii) (B) or (C) of this definition qualify for FMLA leave even though the employee or the immediate family member does not receive treatment from a health care provider during the absence, and even if the absence does not last more than three days. For example, an employee with asthma may be unable to report for work due to the onset of an asthma attack or because the employee's health care provider has advised the employee to stay home when the pollen count exceeds a certain level. An employee who is pregnant may be unable to report to work because of severe morning sickness.

Son or daughter means a biological, adopted, or foster child, a stepchild, a legal ward, or a child of a person standing *in loco parentis*, who is under 18 years of age or 18 years of age or older and incapable of self-care because of a mental or physical disability.

Spouse means a husband or wife as defined or recognized under State law for purposes of marriage in the State where the employee resides, including common law marriage in States where it is recognized.

State means any State of the United States or the District of Columbia or any Territory or possession of the United States.

Teacher (or *employee employed in an instructional capacity*, or *instructional employee*) means an employee employed principally in an instructional capacity by an educational agency or school whose principal function is to teach and instruct students in a class, a small group, or an individual setting, and includes athletic coaches, driving instructors, and special education assistants such as signers for the hearing impaired. The term does not include teacher assistants or aides who do not have as their principal function actual teaching or instructing, nor auxiliary personnel such as counselors, psychologists, curriculum specialists, cafeteria workers, maintenance workers, bus drivers, or other primarily noninstructional employees.

APPENDIX C INDEX

The citations listed in this Appendix are to sections in 29 CFR Part 825.

Parent 825.100(a), 825.101(a),
825.112, 825.113, 825.116(a),
825.200(a), 825.202(a), 825.207(b),
825.213(a), 825.305(a), 825.306(d),
825.800

Physical or mental disability
825.113(c), 825.114, 825.215(b),
825.500(e), 825.800

Placement of a child 825.100(a),
825.201, 825.203(a), 825.207(b)

Postal Rate Commission 825.109(b),
825.800

Posting requirement 825.300,
825.402

Premium payments 825.100(b),
825.210, 825.212, 825.213(f),
825.301(c), 825.308(d), 825.500(c)

Private employer 825.105, 825.108(b)

Public agency 825.104(a), 825.108,
825.109, 825.800

Recertification 825.301(c), 825.308
Records 825.110(c), 825.206(a),
825.500

Reduced leave schedule 825.111(d),
825.114(d), 825.116(c), 825.117,
825.203, 825.205, 825.302(f),
825.306(d), 825.500(c), 825.601,
825.702(c), 825.800

Restoration 825.100(d), 825.106(e),
825.209(g), 825.213(a), 825.216,
825.218, 825.219, 825.301(c),
825.311(c), 825.312

Returning to work 825.214

Right to reinstatement 825.100(c),
825.209(g), 825.214(b),
825.216(a), 825.219, 825.301(c),
825.311(c), 825.312, 825.400,
825.700

Secondary employer 825.106(f)

Serious health condition 825.100,
825.101(a), 825.112(a), 825.114,
825.116(a), 825.200(a),
825.202(a), 825.203, 825.204(a),
825.206(b), 825.207, 825.213,
825.215(b), 825.301(c), 825.302,
825.303, 825.305, 825.306,
825.308(d), 825.310(a),
825.311(c), 825.312(b),
825.601(a), 825.602(a), 825.800

Son or daughter 825.112(a),
825.113(c), 825.202(a), 825.800

Spouse 825.100(a), 825.101(a),
825.112(a), 825.113(a),
825.200(a), 825.202, 825.213(a),
825.303(b), 825.305(a),
825.306(d), 825.701(a), 825.800

State laws 825.701

Substantial and grievous economic
injury 825.213(a), 825.216(c),
825.218, 825.219, 825.312(f)

Successor in interest 825.104(a),
825.107, 825.800

Teacher(s) 825.110(c), 825.600(c),
825.800

U.S. Tax Court 825.109(b)

Unpaid leave 825.100, 825.101(a),
825.105(b), 825.206, 825.208,
825.601(b)

Waive rights 825.220(d)

Workers' compensation
825.207(d)(1), 825.210(f),
825.216(d), 825.307(a)(1),
825.720(d)(1)

Worksite 825.108(d), 825.110(a),
825.111, 825.213(a), 825.214(e),
825.217, 825.220(b), 825.304(c),
825.800

APPENDIX D
OFFICE OF PERSONNEL MANAGEMENT (OPM) REGULATIONS (COVERING FEDERAL EMPLOYEES)
5 C.F.R. §§ 630.1201–1211

PART 630-ABSENCE AND LEAVE

§ 630.1201 Purpose, applicability, and administration.

(a) *Purpose.* This subpart provides regulations to implement sections 6381 through 6387 of title 5, United States Code. This subpart must be read together with those sections of law. Sections 6381 through 6387 of title 5, United States Code, provide a standard approach to providing family and medical leave to Federal employees by prescribing an entitlement to a total of 12 administrative workweeks of unpaid leave during any 12-month period for certain family and medical needs, as specified in § 630.1203(a) of this part.

(b) *Applicability.*

(1) Except as otherwise provided in this paragraph, this subpart applies to any employee who—

(i) Is defined as an "employee" under 5 U.S.C. 6301(2), excluding employees covered under paragraph (b)(2) of this section; and

(ii) Has completed at least 12 months of service (not required to be 12 recent or consecutive months) as—

(A) An employee, as defined under 5 U.S.C. 6301(2), excluding any service as an employee under paragraph (b)(2) of this section;

(B) A physician, dentist, or nurse in the Veterans Health Administration of the Department of Veterans Affairs who is appointed under section 7401(1) of title 38, United States Code;

(C) A "teacher" or an individual holding a "teaching position," as defined in section 901 of title 20, United States Code; or

(D) An employee identified in section 2105(c) of title 5, United States Code, who is paid from nonappropriated funds.

(2) This subpart does not apply to—

(i) An individual employed by the government of the District of Columbia;

OPM REGULATIONS** **113**

(ii) An employee serving under a temporary appointment with a time limitation of 1 year or less;

(iii) An intermittent employee, as defined in 5 CFR 340.401(c); or

(iv) Any employee covered by Title I or Title V of the Family and Medical Leave Act of 1993 (Pub. L. 103-3, February 5, 1993). The Department of Labor has issued regulations implementing Title I at 29 CFR Part 825.

(3) For the purpose of applying sections 6381 through 6387 of title 5, United States Code—

(i) A physician, dentist, or nurse in the Veterans Health Administration of the Department of Veterans Affairs appointed under section 7401(1) of title 38, United States Code, shall be governed by the terms and conditions of regulations prescribed by the Secretary of Veterans Affairs;

(ii) A "teacher" or an individual holding a "teaching position," as defined in section 901 of title 20, United States Code, shall be governed by the terms and conditions of regulations prescribed by the Secretary of Defense; and

(iii) An employee identified in section 2105(c) of title 5, United States Code, who is paid from nonappropriated funds shall be governed by the terms and conditions of regulations prescribed by the Secretary of Defense or the Secretary of Transportation, as appropriate.

(4) The regulations prescribed by the Secretary of Veterans Affairs, Secretary of Defense, or Secretary of Transportation under paragraph (b)(3) of this section shall, to the extent appropriate, be consistent with the regulations prescribed in this subpart and the regulations prescribed by the Secretary of Labor to carry out Title I of the Family and Medical Leave Act of 1993 at 29 CFR Part 825.

(c) *Administration.* The head of an agency having employees subject to this subpart is responsible for the proper administration of this subpart.

§ 630.1202 Definitions.

In this subpart:

Accrued leave has the meaning given that term in § 630.201 of this part.

Accumulated leave has the meaning given that term in § 630.201 of this part.

Administrative workweek has the meaning given that term in § 610.102 of this chapter.

Adoption refers to a legal process in which an individual becomes the legal parent of another's child. The source of an adopted child—*e.g.*, whether from a licensed placement agency or otherwise-is not a factor in determining eligibility for leave under this subpart.

Continuing treatment by a health care provider means one or more of the following situations where an employee or an employee's spouse, son, daughter, or parent—

(1) Is treated two or more times for an illness or injury by a health care provider;

(2) Is treated two or more times for an illness or injury by a health care provider under the orders of, or on referral by, the individual's health care provider or is treated for the illness or injury on at least one occasion which results in a regimen of continuing treatment under the supervision of the health care provider—*e.g.*, a course of medication or therapy—to resolve the health condition; or

(3) Is under the continuing supervision of the health care provider, but may not necessarily be actively treated by the health care provider, due to a serious long-term or chronic condition or disability which cannot be cured-*e.g.*, Alzheimer's disease, severe stroke, or terminal stages of a disease.

Employee means an individual to whom this subpart applies.

Essential functions means the fundamental job duties of the employee's position, as defined in 29 CFR 1630.2.

Family and medical leave means an employee's entitlement to 12 administrative workweeks of unpaid leave for certain family and medical needs, as prescribed under sections 6381 through 6387 of title 5, United States Code.

Foster care means 24-hour care for children in substitution for, and away from, their parents or guardian. Such placement is made by or with the agreement of the State as a result of a voluntary agreement by the parent or guardian that the child be removed from the home, or pursuant to a judicial determination of the necessity for foster care, and involves agreement between the State and foster family to take the child.

Health care provider means—

(1) A licensed Doctor of Medicine or Doctor of Osteopathy or a physician who is serving on active duty in the uniformed services and is designated by the uniformed service to conduct examinations under this subpart;

(2) A person providing health services who is not a medical doctor, but who is certified by a national organization and licensed by a State to provide the service in question; or

(3) A Christian Science practitioner listed with the First Church of Christ, Scientist, in Boston, Massachusetts.

In loco parentis refers to the situation of an individual who has day-to-day responsibility for the care and financial support of a child or, in the case of an employee, who had such responsibility for the employee when the employee was a child. A biological or legal relationship is not necessary.

Intermittent leave or leave taken intermittently means leave taken in separate blocks of time rather than for one continuous period of time, and may include leave periods of less than 1 hour to several weeks.

Leave without pay means an absence from duty in a nonpay status. Leave without pay may be taken only for those hours of duty comprising an employee's basic workweek.

Parent means a biological parent or an individual who stands or stood in loco parentis to an employee when the employee was a child. This term does not include parents "in law."

Reduced leave schedule means a work schedule under which the usual number of hours of regularly scheduled work per workday or workweek of an employee is reduced. The number of hours by which the daily or weekly tour of duty is reduced are counted as leave for the purpose of this subpart.

Regularly scheduled has the meaning given that term in § 610.102 of this chapter.

Regularly scheduled administrative workweek has the meaning given that term in § 610.102 of this chapter.

Serious health condition means an illness, injury, impairment, or physical or mental condition that involves—

(1) Any period of incapacity or treatment in connection with or consequent to inpatient care (*i.e.*, an overnight stay) in a hospital, hospice, or residential medical care facility;

(2) Any period of incapacity requiring absence from work, school, or other regular daily activities, of more than 3 calendar days, that also involves continuing treatment by (or under the supervision of) a health care provider; or

(3) Continuing treatment by (or under the supervision of) a health care provider for a chronic or long-term health condition that is incurable or so serious that, if not treated, would likely result in a period of incapacity of more than 3 calendar days; or for prenatal care.

Son or daughter means a biological, adopted, or foster child; a stepchild; a legal ward; or a child of a person standing in loco parentis who is—

(1) Under 18 years of age; or

(2) 18 years of age or older and incapable of self-care because of a mental or physical disability. A son or daughter incapable of self-care requires active assistance or supervision to provide daily self-care in several of the

"activities of daily living" or "ADLs." Activities of daily living include adaptive activities such as caring appropriately for one's grooming and hygiene, bathing, dressing, eating, cooking, cleaning, shopping, taking public transportation, paying bills, maintaining a residence, using telephones and directories, and using a post office. A mental or physical disability refers to a "disability," as defined in 29 CFR 1630.2(g).

Spouse means a husband or wife, as defined or recognized under State law for purposes of marriage, including common law marriage in States where it is recognized.

Tour of duty has the meaning given that term in § 610.102(h) of this chapter.

§ 630.1203 Leave entitlement.

(a) An employee shall be entitled to a total of 12 administrative workweeks of unpaid leave during any 12-month period for one or more of the following reasons:

(1) The birth of a son or daughter of the employee and the care of such son or daughter;

(2) The placement of a son or daughter with the employee for adoption or foster care;

(3) The care of a spouse, son, daughter, or parent of the employee, if such spouse, son, daughter, or parent has a serious health condition; or

(4) A serious health condition of the employee that makes the employee unable to perform the essential functions of his or her position.

(b) An employee shall take only the amount of family and medical leave that is necessary to manage the circumstance that prompted the need for leave under paragraph (a) of this section.

(c) Except as provided in paragraph (d)(2) of this section, the 12-month period referred to in paragraph (a) of this section begins on the date an employee first takes leave for a family or medical need specified in that paragraph and continues for 12 months. An employee is not entitled to 12 additional workweeks of leave until the previous 12-month period ends and an event or situation occurs that entitles the employee to another period of family or medical leave. (This may include a continuation of a previous situation or circumstance.)

(d) The entitlement to a total of 12 administrative workweeks of leave under paragraphs (a) (1) and (2) of this section—

(1) May begin prior to or on the actual date of birth or placement for adoption or foster care; and

(2) Shall expire 12 months after the date of birth or placement. Leave for a birth or placement must be concluded within 12 months after the date of birth or placement.

(e) Leave under paragraph (a) of this section is available to full-time and part-time employees. A total of 12 administrative workweeks will be made available equally for a full-time or part-time employee in direct proportion to the number of hours in the employee's regularly scheduled administrative workweek. The 12 administrative workweeks of leave will be calculated on an hourly basis and will equal 12 times the average number of hours in the employee's regularly scheduled administrative workweek. If the number of hours in an employee's workweek varies from week to week, a weekly average of the hours scheduled over the 12 weeks prior to the date leave commences shall be used as the basis for this calculation.

(f) If the number of hours in an employee's regularly scheduled administrative workweek is changed during the 12-month period of family and medical leave, the employee's entitlement to any remaining family and medical leave will be recalculated based on the number of hours in the employee's current regularly scheduled administrative workweek.

(g) When an employee requests leave under paragraph (a) of this section, the agency must provide guidance concerning an employee's rights and obligations under this subpart.

(h) An agency may not subtract leave from an employee's entitlement to leave under paragraph (a) of this section unless the agency has obtained confirmation from the employee of his or her intent to invoke entitlement to leave under paragraph (a) of this section. An employee's notice of his or her intent to take leave under § 630.1206 of this part may suffice as the employee's confirmation.

§ 630.1204 Intermittent leave or reduced leave schedule.

(a) Leave under § 630.1203(a) (1) or (2) of this part shall not be taken intermittently or on a reduced leave schedule unless the employee and the agency agree to do so.

(b) Leave under § 630.1203(a) (3) or (4) of this part may be taken intermittently or on a reduced leave schedule when medically necessary, subject to § 630.1206 and 630.1207(b)(6) of this part.

(c) If an employee takes leave under § 630.1203(a) (3) or (4) of this part intermittently or on a reduced leave schedule that is foreseeable based on planned medical treatment or recovery from a serious health condition, the agency may place the employee temporarily in an available alternative position for which the employee is qualified and that can better accommodate recurring periods of leave. Upon returning from leave, the employee shall be entitled to be returned to his or her permanent position or an equivalent position, as provided in § 630.1208(a) of this part.

(d) For the purpose of applying paragraph (c) of this section, an alternative position must be in the same commuting area and must provide—

(1) An equivalent grade or pay level, including any applicable locality-based comparability payment under 5 U.S.C. 5304; special rate of pay for law enforcement officers or special pay adjustment for law enforcement officers under section 403 or 404 of the Federal Employees Pay Comparability Act of 1990 (Pub. L. 101 509), respectively; continued rate of pay under subpart G of part 531 of this chapter; or special salary rate under 5 U.S.C. 5305 or similar provision of law;

(2) The same type of appointment, work schedule, status, and tenure; and

(3) The same employment benefits made available to the employee in his or her previous position (e.g., life insurance, health benefits, retirement coverage, and leave accrual).

(e) The agency shall determine the available alternative position that has equivalent pay and benefits consistent with Federal laws, including the Rehabilitation Act of 1973 (29 U.S.C. 701) and the Pregnancy Discrimination Act of 1978 (42 U.S.C. 2000e).

(f) The number of hours of leave taken intermittently or on a reduced leave schedule shall be subtracted, on an hour-for-hour basis, from the total amount of leave available to the employee under § 630.1203 (e) and (f) of this part.

§ 630.1205 Substitution of paid leave.

(a) Except as provided in paragraph (b) of this section, leave taken under § 630.1203(a) of this part shall be leave without pay.

(b) An employee may elect to substitute the following paid time off for any or all of the period of leave taken under § 630.1203(a) of this part—

(1) Accrued or accumulated annual or sick leave under subchapter I of chapter 63 of title 5, United States Code, consistent with current law and regulations governing the granting and use of annual or sick leave;

(2) Advanced annual or sick leave approved under the same terms and conditions that apply to any other agency employee who requests advanced annual or sick leave;

(3) Leave made available to an employee under the Voluntary Leave Transfer Program or the Voluntary Leave Bank Program consistent with subparts I and J of part 630 of this chapter;

(4) Compensatory time off; and

(5) Credit hours accrued under a flexible work schedule.

(c) An agency may not deny an employee's right to substitute paid time off under paragraph (b) of this section for any or all of the period of leave taken § 630.1203(a) of this part.

(d) An agency may not require an employee to substitute paid time off under paragraph (b) of this section for any or all of the period of leave taken under § 630.1203(a) of this part.

(e) An employee shall notify the agency of his or her intent to substitute paid time off under paragraph (b) of this section for the period of leave to be taken under § 630.1203(a) of this part prior to the date such paid time off commences.

§ 630.1206 Notice of leave.

(a) If leave taken under § 630.1203(a) of this part is foreseeable based on an expected birth, placement for adoption or foster care, or planned medical treatment, the employee shall provide notice to the agency of his or her intention to take leave not less than 30 days before the date the leave is to begin. If the date of birth or placement or planned medical treatment requires leave to begin within 30 days, the employee shall provide such notice as is practicable.

(b) If leave taken under § 630.1203(a) (3) or (4) of this part is foreseeable based on planned medical treatment, the employee shall consult with the agency and make a reasonable effort to schedule medical treatment so as not to disrupt unduly the operations of the agency, subject to the approval of the health care provider. The agency may, for justifiable cause, request that an employee reschedule medical treatment, subject to the approval of the health care provider.

(c) If the need for leave is not foreseeable-*e.g.*, a medical emergency or the unexpected availability of a child for adoption or foster care, and the employee cannot provide 30 days' notice of his or her need for leave, the employee shall provide notice within a reasonable period of time appropriate to the circumstances involved. If necessary, notice may be given by an employee's personal representative (*e.g.*, a family member or other responsible party). If the need for leave is not foreseeable and the employee is unable, due to circumstances beyond his or her control, to provide notice of his or her need for leave, the leave may not be delayed or denied.

(d) If the need for leave is foreseeable, and the employee fails to give 30 days' notice with no reasonable excuse for the delay of notification, the agency may delay the taking of leave under § 630.1203(a) of this part until at least 30 days after the date the employee provides notice of his or her need for family and medical leave.

(e) An agency may waive the notice requirements under paragraph (a) of this section and instead impose the agency's usual and customary policies or procedures for providing notification of leave. The agency's policies or procedures for providing notification of leave must not be more stringent than the requirements in this section. However, an agency may not deny an employee's entitlement to leave under § 630.1203(a) of this part if the employee fails to follow such agency policies or procedures.

(f) An agency may require that a request for leave under § 630.1203(a)(2) of this part be supported by evidence that is administratively acceptable to the agency.

§ 630.1207 Medical certification.

(a) An agency may require that a request for leave under § 630.1203(a) (3) or (4) of this part be supported by written medical certification issued by the health care provider of the employee or the health care provider of the spouse, son, daughter, or parent of the employee, as appropriate. An employee shall provide the written medical certification to the agency in a timely manner.

(b) The written medical certification shall include—
 (1) The date the serious health condition commenced;
 (2) The probable duration of the serious health condition;
 (3) The appropriate medical facts within the knowledge of the health care provider regarding the serious health condition, including a general statement as to the incapacitation, examination, or treatment that may be required by a health care provider;
 (4) For the purpose of leave taken under § 630.1203(a)(3) of this part—
  (i) A statement from the health care provider that the spouse, son, daughter, or parent of the employee requires psychological comfort and/or physical care; needs assistance for basic medical, hygienic, nutritional, safety, or transportation needs or in making arrangements to meet such needs; and would benefit from the employee's care or presence; and
  (ii) A statement from the employee on the care he or she will provide and an estimate of the amount of time needed to care for his or her spouse, son, daughter, or parent;
 (5) For the purpose of leave taken under § 630.1203(a)(4) of this part, a statement that the employee is unable to perform the essential functions of his or her position, based on written information provided by the agency on the essential functions of the employee's position or, if not provided, discussion with the employee about the essential functions of his or her position; and
 (6) In the case of certification for intermittent leave or leave on a reduced leave schedule under § 630.1203(a) (3) or (4) of this part for planned medical treatment, the dates on which such treatment is expected to be given and the duration of such treatment.

(c) The agency shall not require any personal or confidential information in the written medical certification other than that required by paragraph (b) of this section.

(d) If the agency doubts the validity of the original certification provided under paragraph (a) of this section, the agency may require, at the agency's expense, that the employee obtain the opinion of a second health care provider designated or approved by the agency concerning the information certified under paragraph (b) of this section. Any health care provider designated or approved by the agency shall not be employed by the agency or be under the administrative oversight of the agency on a regular basis unless the agency is located in an area where access to health care is extremely limited — *e.g.*, a rural area or an overseas location where no more than one or two health care providers practice in the relevant specialty, or the only health care providers available are employed by the agency.

(e) If the opinion of the second health care provider differs from the original certification provided under paragraph (a) of this section, the agency may require, at the agency's expense, that the employee obtain the opinion of a third health care provider designated or approved jointly by the agency and the employee concerning the information certified under paragraph (b) of this section. The opinion of the third health care provider shall be binding on the agency and the employee.

(f) To remain entitled to family and medical leave under § 630.1203(a) (3) or (4) of this part, an employee or the employee's spouse, son, daughter, or parent must comply with any requirement from an agency that he or she submit to examination (though not treatment) to obtain a second or third medical certification from a health care provider other than the individual's health care provider.

(g) If the employee is unable to provide the requested medical certification before leave begins, or if the agency questions the validity of the original certification provided by the employee and the medical treatment requires the leave to begin, the agency shall grant provisional leave pending final written medical certification.

(h) If, after the leave has commenced, the employee fails to provide the requested medical certification, the agency may—
    (1) Charge the employee as absent without leave (AWOL); or
    (2) Allow the employee to request that the provisional leave be charged as leave without pay or charged to the employee's annual and/or sick leave account, as appropriate.

(i) While an employee is on family and medical leave, the agency may require, at the agency's expense, subsequent medical recertification from the health care provider on a periodic basis, not more often than every 30 calendar days. An agency may require subsequent medical recertification more frequently than every 30 calendar days if the employee requests that the original leave period be extended, the circumstances described in the original medical certification have changed significantly, or the agency receives information that casts doubt upon the continuing validity of the medical certification.

(j) To ensure the security and confidentiality of any written medical certification under § 630.1207 or 630.1208(h) of this part, the medical certification shall be subject to the provisions for safeguarding information about individuals under subpart A or part 293 of this chapter.

§ 630.1208 Protection of employment and benefits.

(a) Any employee who takes leave under § 630.1203(a) of this part shall be entitled, upon return to the agency, to be returned to—

   (1) The same position held by the employee when the leave commenced; or

   (2) An equivalent position with equivalent benefits, pay, status, and other terms and conditions of employment.

(b) For the purpose of applying paragraph (a)(2) of this section, an equivalent position must be in the same commuting area and must carry or provide at a minimum—

   (1) The same or substantially similar duties and responsibilities, which must entail substantially equivalent skill, effort, responsibility, and authority;

   (2) An equivalent grade or pay level, including any applicable locality-based comparability payment under 5 U.S.C. 5304; special rate of pay for law enforcement officers or special pay adjustment for law enforcement officers under section 403 or 404 of the Federal Employees Pay Comparability Act of 1990 (Pub. L. 101 509), respectively; continued rate of pay under subpart G of part 531 of this chapter; or special salary rate under 5 U.S.C. 5305 or similar provision of law;

   (3) The same type of appointment, work schedule, status, and tenure;

   (4) The same employment benefits made available to the employee in his or her previous position (*e.g.*, life insurance, health benefits, retirement coverage, and leave accrual);

   (5) The same or equivalent opportunity for a within-grade increase, merit pay increase, performance award, incentive award, or other similar discretionary and non-discretionary payments consistent with applicable laws and regulations;

   (6) The same or equivalent opportunity for premium pay consistent with applicable law and regulations under 5 CFR Part 550, subpart A, or 5 CFR Part 551, subpart E; and

(7) The same or equivalent opportunity for training or education benefits consistent with applicable laws and regulations, including any training that an employee may be required to complete to qualify for his or her previous position.

(c) As a result of taking leave under § 630.1203(a) of this part, an employee shall not suffer the loss of any employment benefit accrued prior to the date on which the leave commenced.

(d) Except as otherwise provided by or under law, a restored employee shall not be entitled to—

(1) The accrual of any employment benefits during any period of leave; or

(2) Any right, benefit, or position of employment other than any right, benefit, or position to which the employee would have been entitled had the employee not taken the leave.

(e) For the purpose of applying paragraph (d) of this section, the same entitlements and limitations in law and regulations that apply to the position, pay, benefits, status, and other terms and conditions of employment of an employee in a leave without pay status shall apply to any employee taking leave without pay under this part, except where different entitlements and limitations are specifically provided in this subpart.

(f) An employee is not entitled to be returned to the same or equivalent position under paragraph (a) of this section if the employee would not otherwise have been employed in that position at the time the employee returns from leave.

(g) An agency may not return an employee to an equivalent position where written notification has been provided that the equivalent position will be affected by a reduction in force if the employee's previous position is not affected by a reduction in force.

(h) As a condition to returning an employee who takes leave under § 630.1203(a)(4) of this part, an agency may establish a uniformly applied practice or policy that requires an employee to obtain written medical certification from the health care provider of the employee that the employee is able to perform the essential functions of his or her position. An agency's policy or practice to require written medical certification attesting to an employee's recovery from a serious health condition shall apply only to those employees in positions that have specific medical standards, physical requirements, or who are covered by a medical evaluation program, as provided under 5 CFR Part 339. Consistent with 5 CFR 339.301, the written medical certification shall be limited to documentation necessary to prove that the employee meets the specific physical qualifications and/or medical standards for his or her position.

(i) If an agency requires an employee to obtain written medical certification under paragraph (h) of this section before he or she returns to work, the agency shall notify each employee of this requirement before leave commences and pay the expenses for obtaining the written medical certification. An employee's refusal to provide written medical certification under paragraph (h) of this section is grounds for appropriate disciplinary or adverse action, as provided in 5 CFR 339.102(c).

(j) An agency may require an employee to report periodically to the agency on his or her status and intention to return to work. An agency's policy requiring such reports must take into account all of the relevant facts and circumstances of the employee's situation.

§ 630.1209 Health benefits.

An employee enrolled in a health benefits plan under the Federal Employees Health Benefits Program (established under chapter 89 of title 5, United States Code) who is placed in a leave without pay status as a result of entitlement to leave under § 630.1203(a) of this part may continue his or her health benefits enrollment while in the leave without pay status and arrange to pay the appropriate employee contributions into the Employees Health Benefits Fund (established under section 8909 of title 5, United States Code). The employee shall make such contributions consistent with 5 CFR 890.502.

§ 630.1210 Greater leave entitlements.

(a) An agency shall comply with any collective bargaining agreement or any agency employment benefit program or plan that provides greater family or medical leave entitlements to employees than those provided under this subpart.

(b) The entitlements established for employees under this subpart may not be diminished by any collective bargaining agreement or any employment benefit program or plan.

(c) An agency may adopt leave policies more generous that those provided in this subpart, except that such policies may not provide entitlement to paid time off greater than that otherwise authorized by law or provide sick leave in any situation in which sick leave would not normally be allowed by law or regulation.

(d) The entitlements under sections 6381 through 6387 of title 5, United States Code, and this subpart do not modify or affect any Federal law prohibiting discrimination. If the entitlements under sections 6381 through 6387 of title 5, United States Code, and this subpart conflict with any Federal law prohibiting discrimination, an agency must comply with whichever statute provides greater entitlements to employees.

§ 630.1211 Records and reports.

(a) So that OPM can evaluate the use of family and medical leave by Federal employees and provide the Congress and others with information about the use of this entitlement, each agency shall maintain records on employees who take leave under this subpart and submit to OPM such records and reports as OPM may require.

(b) At a minimum, each agency shall maintain the following information concerning each employee who takes leave under this subpart:

(1) The employee's rate of basic pay, as defined in 5 CFR 550.103;

(2) The occupational series for the employee's position;

(3) The number of hours of leave taken under § 630.1203(a) of this part; and

(4) Whether leave was taken—

(i) Under § 630.1203(a) (1), (2) or (3) of this part; or

(ii) Under § 630.1203(a)(4) of this part.

(c) When an employee transfers to a different agency, the losing agency shall provide the gaining agency with information on leave taken under § 630.1203(a) of this part by the employee during the 12 months prior to the date of transfer. The losing agency shall provide the following information:

(1) The beginning and ending dates of the employee's 12-month period, as determined under § 630.1203(c) of this part; and

(2) The number of hours of leave taken under § 630.1203(a) of the part during the employee's 12-month period, as determined under § 630.1203(c) of this part.

APPENDIX E

DOL FORM FOR CERTIFICATION OF HEALTH CARE PROVIDER (OPTIONAL FORM WH-380)

Certification of Health Care Provider (Family and Medical Leave Act of 1993)	**U.S. Department of Labor** Employment Standards Administration Wage and Hour Division
1. Employee's Name	2. Patient's Name (if different from employee)

3. The attached sheet describes what is meant by a **"serious health condition"** under the Family and Medical Leave Act. Does the patient's condition qualify under any of the categories described? If so, please check the applicable category.

(1) _____ (2) _____ (3) _____ (4) _____ (5) _____ (6) _____ , or None of the above _____

4. Describe the **medical facts** which support your certification, including a brief statement as to how the medical facts meet the criteria of one of these categories:

5.a. State the approximate **date** the condition commenced, and the probable **duration** of the condition (and also the probable duration of the patient's **incapacity**[2] if different):

   b. Will it be necessary for the employee to work only **intermittently or to work on a less than full schedule** as a result of the condition (including for treatment described in Item 6 below)? _____

If yes, give the probable duration:

   c. If the condition is a **chronic condition** (condition #4) or **pregnancy**, state whether the patient is presently incapacitated[2] and the likely duration and frequency of **episodes of incapacity**[2]:

6.a. If additional treatments will be required for the condition, provide an estimate of the probable number of such treatments:

If the patient will be absent from work or other daily activities because of **treatment** on an **intermittent** or **part-time** basis, also provide an estimate of the probably number and interval between such treatments, actual or estimated dates of treatment if known, and period required for recovery if any:

   b. If any of these treatments will be provided by **another provider of health services** (e.g., physical therapist), please state the nature of the treatments:

---

[1] Here and elsewhere on this form, the information sought relates **only** to the condition for which the employee is taking FMLA leave.

[2] **Incapacity,"** for purposes of FMLA, is defined to mean inability to work, attend school or perform other regular daily activities due to the serious health condition, treatment therefor, or recovery therefrom.

Form WH-380
March 1995

1

c. **If a regimen of continuing treatment** by the patient is required under your supervision, provide a general description of such regimen (e.g., prescription drugs, physical therapy requiring special equipment):

7.a. If medical leave is required for the employee's **absence from work** because of the **employee's own condition** (including absences due to pregnancy or a chronic condition), is the employee **unable to perform work** of any kind? _____

b. If able to perform some work, is the employee **unable to perform any one or more of the essential functions of the employee's job** (the employee or the employer should supply you with information about the essential job functions)? _____ If yes, please list the essential functions the employee is unable to perform:

c. If neither a. nor b. applies, is it necessary for the employee to be **absent from work for treatment?** _____

8a. If leave is required to **care for a family member** of the employee with a serious health condition, **does the patient require assistance** for basic medical or personal needs or safety, or for transportation? _____

b. If no, would the employee's presence to provide **psychological comfort** be beneficial to the patient or assist in the patient's recovery? _____

c. If the patient will need care only **intermittently** or on a part-time basis, please indicate the probable duration of this need:

_____   _____
(Signature of Health Care Provider)   (Type of Practice)

_____   _____
(Address)   (Telephone number)

To be completed by the employee needing family leave to care for a family member:

State the care you will provide and an estimate of the period during which care will be provided, including a schedule if leave is to be taken intermittently or if it will be necessary for you to work less than a full schedule:

_____   _____
(Employee Signature)   (Date)

2

A **"Serious Health Condition"** means an illness, injury impairment, or physical or mental condition that involves one of the following:

1. Hospital Care

Inpatient care (*i.e.,* an overnight stay) in a hospital, hospice, or residential medical care facility, including any period of incapacity[2] or subsequent treatment in connection with or consequent to such inpatient care.

2. Absence Plus Treatment

(a) A period of incapacity[2] of **more than three consecutive calendar days** (including any subsequent treatment or period of incapacity[2] relating to the same condition), that also involves:

(1) **Treatment[3] two or more times** by a health care provider, by a nurse or physician's assistant under direct supervision of a health care provider, or by a provider of health care services (*e.g.,* physical therapist) under orders of, or on referral by, a health care provider; or

(2) **Treatment** by a health care provider on **at least one occasion** which results in a **regimen of continuing treatment[4]** under the supervision of the health care provider.

3. Pregnancy

Any period of incapacity due to **pregnany,** or for **prenatal care.**

4. Chronic Conditions Requiring Treatments

A **chronic condition** which:

(1) Requires **periodic visits** for treatment by a health care provider, or by a nurse or physician's assistant under direct supervision of a health care provider;

(2) Continues over an **extended period of time** (including recurring episodes of a single underlying condition); and

(3) May cause **episodic** rather than a continuing period of incapacity[2] (e.g., asthma, diabetes, epilepsy, etc.).

5. Permanent/Long-term Conditions Requiring Supervision

A period of **incapacity[2]** which is **permanent or long-term** due to a condition for which treatment may not be effective. The employee or family member must be **under the continuing supervision of, but need not be receiving active treatment by, a health care provider.** Examples include Alzheimer's, a severe stroke, or the terminal stages of a disease.

---

3   Treatment includes examinations to determine if a serious health condition exists and evaluations of the condition. Treatment does not include routine physical examinations, eye examinations, or dental examinations.

4   A regimen of continuing treatment includes, for example, a course of prescription medication (e.g., an antibiotic) or therapy requiring special equipment to resolve or alleviate the health condition. A regimen of treatment does not include the taking of over-the-counter medications such as aspirin, antihistamines, or salves; or bed-rest, drinking fluids, exercise, and other similar activities that can be initiated without a visit to a health care provider.

3

6. Multiple Treatments (Non-Chronic Conditions)

Any period of absence to receive **multiple treatments** (including any period of recovery therefrom) by a health care provider or by a provider of health care services under orders of, or on referral by. a health care provider, either for **restorative surgery** after an accident or other injury, **or** for a condition that **would likely result in a period of incapacity[2] of more than three consecutive calendar days in the absence of medical intervention or treatment,** such as cancer (chemotherapy, radiation, etc.), severe arthritis (physical therapy), kidney disease (dialysis).

4

APPENDIX F
DOL FMLA POSTER

Your Rights
Under The
Family and Medical Leave Act of 1993

FMLA requires covered employers to provide up to 12 weeks of unpaid job-protected leave to "eligible" employees for certain family and medical reasons. Employees are eligible if they have worked for a covered employer for at least one year, and for 1,250 hours over the previous 12 months, and if there are at least 50 employees within 75 miles.

Reasons For Taking Leave:

Unpaid leave must be granted for *any* of the following reasons:

- to care for the employee's child after birth, or placement for adoption or foster care;
- to care for the employee's spouse, son or daughter, or parent, who has a serious health condition; or
- for a serious health condition that makes the employee unable to perform the employee's job.

At the employee's or employer's option, certain kinds of paid leave may be substituted for unpaid leave.

Advance Notice and Medical Certification

The employee may be required to provide advance leave notice and medical certification. Taking of leave may be denied if requirements are not met.

- The employee ordinarily must provide 30 days advance notice when the leave is "foreseeable."
- An employer may require medical certification to support a request for leave because of a serious health condition, and may require second or third opinions (at the employer's expense) and a fitness for duty report to return to work.

Job Benefits and Protection:

- For the duration of FMLA leave, the employer must maintain the employee's health coverage under any "group health plan."

- Upon return from FMLA leave, most employees must be restored to their original or equivalent positions with equivalent pay, benefits, and other employment terms.
- The use of FMLA leave cannot result in the loss of any employment benefit that accrued prior to the start of an employee's leave.

Unlawful Acts By Employers:

FMLA makes it unlawful for any employer to:

- interfere with, restrain, or deny the exercise of any right provided under FMLA:
- discharge or discriminate against any person for opposing any practice made unlawful by FMLA or for involvement in any proceeding under or relating to FMLA.

Enforcement:

- The U.S. Department of Labor is authorized to investigate and resolve complaints of violations.
- An eligible employee may bring a civil action against an employer for violations.

FMLA does not affect any Federal or State law prohibiting discrimination, or supersede any State or local law or collective bargaining agreement which provides greater family or medical leave rights.

For Additional Information:

Contact the nearest office of the Wage and Hour Division, listed in most telephone directories under U.S. Government, Department of Labor.

U.S. Department of Labor
Employment Standards Administration
Wage and Hour Division
Washington, D.C. 20210

WH Publication 1420
June 1993

APPENDIX G

DOL PROTOTYPE EMPLOYER NOTICE: RESPONSE TO EMPLOYEE REQUEST FOR FMLA LEAVE

Employer Response to Employee
Request for Family or Medical Leave
(Optional use form - see 29 CFR § 825.301

U.S. Department of Labor
Employment Standards Administration
Wage and Hour Division

(Family and Medical Leave Act of 1993)

(Date)

TO: _____
(Employee s Name)

FROM: _____
(Name of appropriate employer representative)

SUBJECT: Request for Family/Medical Leave

On _____, you notified us of your need to take family/medical leave due to:
(Date)

☐ the birth of a child, or the placement of a child with you for adoption or foster care; or

☐ a serious health condition that makes you unable to perform the essential functions of your job; or

☐ a serious health condition affecting your ☐ spouse, ☐ child, ☐ parent, for which you are needed to provide care.

You notified us that you need this leave beginning on _____ and that you expect leave to continue until on
or about _____ .   *(date)*
                     (date)

Except as explained below, you have a right under the FMLA for up to 12 weeks of unpaid leave in a l 2-month
period for the reasons listed above. Also, your health benefits must be maintained during any period of unpaid
leave under the same conditions as if you continued to work, and you must be reinstated to the same or an
equivalent job with the same pay, benefits, and terms and conditions of employment on your return from leave.
If you do not return to work following FMLA leave for a reason other than; (1) the continuation, recurrence, or
onset of a serious health condition which would entitle you to FMLA leave; or (2) other circumstances beyond
your control, you may be required to reimburse us for our share of health insurance premiums paid on your
behalf during your FMLA leave.

This is to inform you that: *(check appropriate boxes; explain where Indicated)*

l . You are ☐ eligible   ☐ not eligible   for leave under the FMLA.

2. The requested leave ☐ will   ☐ will not   be counted against your annual FMLA leave entitlement.

3. You ☐ will   ☐ will not   be required to furnish medical certification of a serious health condition. If
   required, you must furnish certification by _____ *(insert date)* (must be at least 15 days after
   you are notified of this requirement) or we may delay the commencement of your leave until the
   certification is submitted.

Form WH-381
March 1995

2

4.   You may elect to substitute accrued paid leave for unpaid FMLA leave. We ☐ will ☐ will not   require that you substitute accrued paid leave for unpaid FMLA leave. If paid leave will be used, the following conditions will apply: *(Explain)*

5(a).   If you normally pay a portion of the premiums for your health insurance, these payments will continue during the period of FMLA leave. Arrangements for payment have been discussed with you and it is agreed that you will make premium payments as follows: *(Set forth dates, e.g., the 10th of each month, or pay periods, etc that specifically cover the agreement with the employee.)*

(b)   You have a minimum 30-day (*or, indicate longer period, if applicable*) grace period in which to make premium payments. If payment is not made timely, your group health insurance may be cancelled, provided we notify you in writing at least 15 days before the date that your health coverage will lapse, or, at our option, we may pay your share of the premiums during FMLA leave, and recover these payments from you upon your return to work. We ☐ will ☐ will not   pay your share of health insurance premiums while you are on leave.

(c)   We ☐ will ☐ will not   do the same with other benefits (e.g., life insurance, disability insurance, etc.) while you are on FMLA leave. If we do pay your premiums for other benefits, when you return from leave you ☐ will ☐ will not   be expected to reimburse us for the payments made on your behalf.

6.   You ☐ will ☐ will not   be required to present a fitness-for-duty certificate prior to being restored to employment. If such certification is required but not received, your return to work may be delayed until certification is provided.

7(a).   You ☐ are ☐ are not   a "key employee" as described in § 825.218 of the FMLA regulations. If you are a "key employee," restoration to employment may be denied following FMLA leave on the grounds that such restoration will cause substantial and grievous economic injury to us.

(b)   We ☐ have ☐ have not   determined that restoring you to employment at the conclusion of FMLA leave will cause substantial and grievous economic harm to us. *(Explain (a) and/or (b) below. See § 825 219 of the FMLA regulations.J*

8.   While on leave, you ☐ will ☐ will not   be required to furnish us with periodic reports every _____ (*indicate interval of periodic reports, as appropriate for the particular leave situation*) of your status and intent to return to work (*see § 825.309 of the FMLA regulations*). If the circumstances of your leave change and you are able to return to work earlier than the date indicated on the reverse side of this form, you ☐ will ☐ will not   be required to notify us at least two work days prior to the date you intend to report for work.

9.   You ☐ will ☐ will not   be required to furnish recertification relating to a serious health condition. *(Explain below, if necessary), including the interval between certifications as prescribed in § 825.308 of the FMLA regulations.)*

B O O K   O R D E R   F O R M

Please send me:

_____ copies of *The FMLA Handbook: A Practical Guide to the Family and Medical Leave Act for Union Members and Stewards* by Robert M. Schwartz

_____ copies of *The Legal Rights of Union Stewards* (English edition) by Robert M. Schwartz

_____ copies of *The Legal Rights of Union Stewards* (Spanish edition) by Robert M. Schwartz

_____ copies of *How to Win Past Practice Grievances* by Robert M. Schwartz

All books are $9.95 per copy. Shipping expenses are $2.00 for the first copy and $.50 each for each additional copy, up to a maximum of $7.00.

Total enclosed: $ _____.

_____

name

_____

address

_____

Mail to: Work Rights Press
               Box 391887
               Cambridge, MA 02139-0008

Bulk rates for orders of 25 or more available upon request.

Telephone: 1-800-576-4552